Democracy, Expertise, and Academic Freedom

ROBERT C. POST

Democracy, Expertise, *and* Academic Freedom

A FIRST AMENDMENT
JURISPRUDENCE FOR THE
MODERN STATE

Yale UNIVERSITY PRESS

New Haven and London

Yale University Press books may be purchased in quantity
for educational, business, or promotional use. For information, please e-mail sales.press@yale.edu (U.S. office) or
sales@yaleup.co.uk (U.K. office).

Set in Bulmer type by Integrated Publishing Solutions.
Printed in the United States of America.

Library of Congress Cataloging-in-Publication Data

Post, Robert, 1947–
Democracy, expertise, and academic freedom :
a First Amendment jurisprudence for the modern state /
Robert C. Post.
p.   cm.
Includes index.
ISBN 978-0-300-14863-3 (hardback)
1. Freedom of speech—United States. 2. United States.
Constitution. 1st Amendment. 3. Academic freedom—
United States. I. Title.
KF4772.P67 2012
342.7308'53—dc23   2011025711

A catalogue record for this book is available from the
British Library.
This paper meets the requirements of ANSI/NISO
Z39.48–1992 (Permanence of Paper).

10 9 8 7 6 5 4 3 2 1

Contents

For Owen:
Il Miglior Fabbro
With affection.

Acknowledgments

This book developed out of the Julius Rosenthal Lectures, which were delivered at Northwestern University School of Law on April 16–18, 2008. I am greatly indebted to the Dean and Faculty of that school for inviting me to join the distinguished list of Rosenthal Lecturers, for their gracious hospitality, and for their valuable comments and suggestions.

I have also been blessed with the insight and critique of many colleagues, to whom I am deeply indebted: Bruce Ackerman, Ed Baker, Vince Blasi, Peter Byrne, Jules Coleman, Matthew Finkin, Owen Fiss, Kent Greenawalt, Philip Hamburger, David Hollinger, Martha Minow, David Rabban, Martin Redish, Jed Rubenfeld, Joan Scott, Scott Shapiro, Michael Siebecker, Reva Siegel, Norman Silber, Peter Strauss, William Van Alstyne, and Jim Weinstein, and for the outstanding research assistance of Jennifer Bishop, Thomas Donnelly, Jacob Gardener, Nathaniel Gleicher, Thomas Schmidt, and David Tannenbaum.

Introduction

As I type these words, I gaze out at my backyard, and I know that there is a large oak in the northwest corner of my lawn. I have knowledge of this oak both because I can see the tree and because I have reason to trust my senses. My knowledge of this oak should be contrasted to my knowledge that cigarettes cause cancer. I cannot acquire the latter form of knowledge merely by observing the world and by trusting my senses.

In fact I have learned about the carcinogenic properties of cigarettes by studying the conclusions of those whom I have reason to trust. We call such persons "experts." How did these experts come to know that cigarettes are carcinogenic? Certainly not in the same way that I came to know about my oak tree. They instead deployed the full and elaborate apparatus of modern epidemiological and statistical science. This science consists of practices of knowing that can be acquired only through training and instruction. The practices create forms of knowledge that are constantly expanding through speculation, observation, analysis, and experiment. In this book I shall refer to this kind of knowledge as "expert" or "disciplinary" knowledge. Any modern society needs expert knowledge in order to survive and prosper.

In this book I analyze the relationship between the First

Amendment and the practices that create and sustain disciplinary knowledge. The bald words of the First Amendment provide that "Congress shall make no law . . . abridging the freedom of speech." We have traditionally interpreted these words to mean that the Constitution protects a "marketplace of ideas"[1] that we believe produces knowledge. This account of the First Amendment was first articulated by Justice Holmes in his justly famous dissent in *Abrams v. United States*,[2] arguably the origin of all judicial efforts to theorize the First Amendment.[3] Holmes explained:

> But when men have realized that time has upset many fighting faiths, they may come to believe even more than they believe the very foundations of their own conduct that the ultimate good desired is better reached by free trade in ideas—that the best test of truth is the power of the thought to get itself accepted in the competition of the market, and that truth is the only ground upon which their wishes safely can be carried out. That at any rate is the theory of our Constitution. It is an experiment, as all life is an experiment.[4]

The United States Supreme Court has since frequently proclaimed that "it is the purpose of the First Amendment to preserve an uninhibited marketplace of ideas in which truth will ultimately prevail."[5] That the point of First Amendment doctrine is to "advance knowledge and the search for truth by fostering a free marketplace of ideas and an 'uninhibited, robust, wide-open debate on public issues'"[6] has become more or less a constitutional commonplace.[7] Indeed, "the most influential argument supporting the constitutional commitment to freedom of speech is the contention that speech is valuable because it leads to the discovery of truth."[8]

The very concept of a marketplace of ideas has long been subject to devastating objections based upon its various imperfections, inefficiencies, and internal contradictions.[9] But in this book I focus on the marketplace of ideas from a slightly different angle. I inquire into the relationship between the marketplace of ideas and the production of expert knowledge. I argue that such knowledge can be produced only if the norms and practices of a discipline are observed.[10] And a discipline, as the *Oxford English Dictionary* reminds us, refers to "the training of scholars or subordinates to proper and orderly action by instructing and exercising them."

The marketplace of ideas expresses the egalitarian principle that persons cannot be regulated based upon the content of their ideas. We have interpreted the First Amendment to mean that every person has an equal right to speak as he or she thinks right. The state is therefore constitutionally prohibited from disciplining our communication on the basis of an official view about what is proper or correct. The First Amendment stands for the proposition that we are not the students of the state. We are adults who are constitutionally empowered to speak for ourselves.

If expert knowledge depends upon the preservation of disciplines, and if disciplines require maintenance of "proper and orderly action," the very independence jealously safeguarded by the First Amendment is in tension with the production of expert knowledge. If we wish to know whether

cigarettes are carcinogenic or whether high tariffs produce
market inefficiencies or whether plutonium-239 has a half-life
of about 24,000 years, we cannot intelligently speak for ourselves. We cannot know such matters by reference to our own
immediate sensual knowledge. We must instead rely on the
results of the disciplinary practices that define atomic physics
or economics or medicine.[11] Anyone who has ever submitted
a paper to a top-flight professional journal would immediately
recognize that these disciplinary practices exclude as much
speech as they facilitate. If a marketplace of ideas model were
to be imposed upon *Nature* or the *American Economic Review*
or *The Lancet,* we would very rapidly lose track of whatever
expertise we possess about the nature of the world.[12]

Contemporary technical expertise is created by practices
that demand *both* critical freedom to inquire *and* affirmative
disciplinary virtues of methodological care, virtues which the
philosopher Charles Peirce once called the "method of science" as distinct from the "method of authority."[13] The maintenance of these virtues quite contradicts the egalitarian toler-
ance that defines the marketplace of ideas paradigm of the
First Amendment. Because the practices that produce expert
knowledge regulate the autonomy of individual speakers to
communicate, because they transpire in venues quite distant
from the sites where democratic public opinion is forged, they
seem estranged from most contemporary theories of the First
Amendment. My object in this book is to inquire what, if anything, can be said about this constitutional hiatus.

I stage this inquiry in three chapters. In Chapter One, I
present what I regard as the most convincing account of the
normative foundations of our First Amendment. This account

centers on the value of what I call "democratic legitimation," which explains why the First Amendment is committed to the egalitarian premise that every person is entitled to communicate his own opinion. In Chapter Two, I discuss the tension between this entitlement and indicia of reliability that define expert knowledge. I argue that there is indeed a First Amendment principle capable of sustaining the disciplinary practices that produce expert knowledge and that this principle depends upon the constitutional value I call "democratic competence." Understanding the relationship between democratic legitimation and democratic competence is difficult and challenging, because democratic legitimation both requires democratic competence and is in many ways incompatible with it. In Chapter Three, I address the consequences of democratic competence for the production of disciplinary knowledge within universities. I discuss the constitutional foundations of academic freedom, which have been badly misunderstood by many contemporary commentators and court decisions. Finally, in the Conclusion, I underscore the larger theoretical implications of the vision of constitutionalism that I espouse.

1

Democratic Legitimation and the First Amendment

In this book I consider the First Amendment as a source of judicially enforced rights. The First Amendment serves this function by establishing distinctive doctrinal tests and standards that courts use to evaluate the constitutionality of government regulations. Following Frederick Schauer, I distinguish between First Amendment "coverage" and First Amendment "protection."[1] The former refers to the kinds of government regulation that should be subject to the special scrutiny exemplified by the distinctive doctrinal tests of the First Amendment; the latter refers to the content of these tests, which determines what courts will allow and what they will forbid. An essential task of First Amendment theory is to explain the scope of First Amendment coverage. We need to know the circumstances in which courts are authorized to deploy the distinctive doctrinal tests and principles of the First Amendment.

The text of the First Amendment refers to "freedom of speech." This has suggested to some, like Justice Souter, "that speech *as such* is subject to some level of protection unless it falls within a category, such as obscenity, placing it beyond the

Amendment's scope."[2] To extend First Amendment coverage to "speech as such" requires an account of what we mean by "speech." Normally any such account begins by distinguishing "speech" from "action." Thus the pioneering First Amendment theorist Thomas Emerson sought to explain the scope of First Amendment coverage by reference to "a fundamental distinction" between "'expression' and 'action,'" a distinction that he believed would have to make up "a crucial ingredient" of any First Amendment theory.[3]

Of course we all can recognize paradigmatic examples of speech and action. Addressing the assembled crowd in Hyde Park is speech; throwing a brick through my neighbor's window is action. But if we try to generalize these paradigmatic examples into systematic principles that distinguish speech from action, we at once run into notorious difficulties. Emerson, for example, sought to define speech as the "communication of ideas."[4] His approach was subsequently adopted by the Supreme Court in *Spence v. Washington,* which held that First Amendment coverage would be triggered whenever "an intent to convey a particularized message was present, and in the surrounding circumstances the likelihood was great that the message would be understood by those who viewed it."[5]

Unfortunately this approach is impossible to reconcile with our actual First Amendment jurisprudence. Even if I throw a brick through my neighbor's window in order to communicate the particularized message that I do not like his religion and that he ought immediately to vacate the premises, and even if the likelihood is great that this message will be understood by my neighbor, no one would think to extend First Amendment coverage to my subsequent prosecution for vandalism.[6] It is child's play to multiply such examples. Just think of all the messages deliberately and successfully conveyed by acts of terrorism.

Moreover First Amendment coverage does *not* extend to large patches of perfectly ordinary state legislation, like the Uniform Commercial Code or the imposition of tort liability for the negligent failure to warn, even though such legislation precisely seeks to control the successful communication of particularized messages in language. "We are men," Montaigne writes, "and we have relations with one another only by speech."[7] To define First Amendment coverage by reference to communication in language would constitutionalize virtually all our "relations with one another," and such a conclusion would be neither accurate nor desirable.

To make matters even more complicated, First Amendment coverage has properly been held to extend to a communication that forms part of a "significant medium for the communication of ideas"[8] even if the communication does *not* succeed in conveying a particularized message.[9] The Court, per Justice Souter, recognized in the context of a St. Patrick's Day parade that if the *Spence* requirement of "a narrow, succinctly articulable message" were taken as precondition for First Amendment coverage, constitutional doctrine "would never reach the unquestionably shielded painting of Jackson Pollock, music of Arnold Schoenberg, or Jabberwocky verse of Lewis Carroll."[10]

These examples suffice to demonstrate that it is not possible constitutionally to distinguish speech from action on the ground that the former communicates ideas or uses language. The implication of this conclusion is quite significant, for it suggests that speech cannot be distinguished from action because of some common property that "speech" possesses but that "action" does not.[11] It follows that the scope of First Amendment coverage cannot be determined merely by observing properties in the world; it does not depend upon the distribution of any natural thing like "ideas" or "speech as such."

Time and again Emerson's efforts to define the scope of First Amendment coverage were frustrated by this fact.[12] But because he was a great First Amendment theorist, one can discern in Emerson's work the seeds of a very different approach to the problem we are considering. Almost casually Emerson notes that the scope of First Amendment coverage may have to be ascertained in light of "the fundamental purposes of the system [of freedom of expression] and the dynamics of its operation."[13] This approach would constitute the polar opposite of *Spence* and the concept of "speech as such." It would determine the reach of First Amendment doctrine not by observing properties of the world—by asking whether regulated behavior communicates ideas—but instead by articulating the purposes of the First Amendment and by developing First Amendment doctrine in ways that serve these purposes. Forms of conduct that realize distinctively First Amendment values would be classified as "speech" that triggers First Amendment coverage.

We can now begin to appreciate why the question of First Amendment coverage is so profound. The actual contours of First Amendment doctrine cannot be explained merely by facts in the world; they must instead reflect the law's efforts to achieve constitutional values. This suggests that we can learn the purposes we have constructed First Amendment doctrine to achieve by tracing the contours of actual First Amendment coverage.[14]

I.

The text of the First Amendment is mute about its purposes. These must be constructed. Judicial efforts to determine the objectives of the First Amendment are less than a century old. Modern First Amendment doctrine first appears in the great Holmes opinions of 1919,[15] and it does not begin to develop until the 1930s. Both the Court and commentators have ever since vigorously debated what the purposes of the First Amendment ought to be.

All Americans are entitled freely to advocate whatever theory of the First Amendment they find most convincing. But when we speak of the purposes of the First Amendment, we refer to the collective allegiances of the nation, in which are rooted the ground and legitimacy of constitutional law. These allegiances become visible in the historical commitments of the judicially enforced First Amendment. To determine the purposes of the First Amendment, therefore, we must consult the actual shape of entrenched First Amendment jurisprudence.

We need not passively receive this inheritance. We can instead aspire to what John Rawls has termed "considered judgment in reflective equilibrium."[16] We can give our nation's actual jurisprudential commitments, as expressed in its historically decided cases, their most powerful, defensible, and persuasive formulation, and we can then critically re-evaluate received doctrine in light of this formulation. Reflective equilibrium requires a critical engagement with our own past. Constitutional law depends upon such engagement because "how we are able to constitute ourselves is profoundly tied to how we are already constituted by our own distinctive history."[17]

Over the past decades, and speaking roughly, three major purposes for the First Amendment have been proposed. The first, embodied in the marketplace of ideas theory, is cognitive; the purpose of First Amendment protections for speech is said to be "advancing knowledge and discovering truth."[18] The second is ethical; the purpose of the First Amendment is said to be "assuring individual self-fulfillment" so that every person can realize his or her "character and potentialities as a human being."[19] And the third is political; the purpose of the First Amendment is said to be facilitating the communicative processes necessary for successful democratic self-governance.[20]

Without question the marketplace of ideas theory captures something essential to growth of knowledge. Kant famously grounded enlightenment in the spirit of *Sapere aude*: the "resolution and courage to use one's own understanding without the guidance of another."[21] The marketplace of ideas theory stresses that knowledge cannot grow, and truth cannot advance, unless the law allows us to venture our own ideas and reasons. Yet when we speak of "advancing knowledge and discovering truth," at least in the context of expert knowledge, we refer to something more than mere hypothesis and speculation.

"Standard analysis" in philosophy holds that "knowledge" is "belief that is both true and justified."[22] Philosophers have puzzled forever about how true and justified belief should be identified, so that "no clear account of knowledge emerges as an established, widely accepted philosophical finding."[23] It does not seem helpful for constitutional lawyers to venture into this epistemological thicket. It would seem rather more useful to affirm, with Allan Gibbard, that "the concept of knowing serves to guide us in relying on some kinds of judgment and not on others."[24] Concluding that a person "knows, then, amounts to planning to rely on his judgment."[25] The question is thus whether the marketplace of ideas gives us grounds to plan to rely on the judgment of others.

There are some who suggest that "human knowledge" should be conceived as simply an endless aggregation of "dispersed information."[26] The challenge is to efficiently and comprehensively assemble relevant data. In this way "Biology, chemistry, physics, economics, psychology, linguistics, history, and many other fields are easily seen as large wikis, in which existing entries, reflecting the stock of knowledge, are 'edited' all the time."[27] Those who favor this approach point to the remarkable success of open source software or prediction markets in "pooling information" to answer questions like whether "the economy of Saudi Arabia [will] prosper in next year."[28] The assumption seems to be that the world will speak for itself so long as we are able to amass the universe of pertinent information.

It would seem implausible, however, if not downright perverse, to seek to determine the half-life of plutonium-239 merely by creating a prediction market, or to ascertain whether cigarettes are carcinogenic by creating a universal wiki.[29] What counts as relevant information in such matters is itself the result of sophisticated disciplinary expertise. We construct relevant data by actively intervening in the world through research, theory, and experiment. Note that Wikipedia itself strictly prohibits the publication of "original research or original thought,"[30] thus distinguishing between readily available information and information produced by the application of disciplinary standards. Wikipedia makes the same (unelucidated) distinction when it provides that "the threshold for inclusion in Wikipedia is **verifiability, not truth**—that is, whether readers are able to check that material added to Wikipedia has already been published by a reliable source, not whether we think it is true."[31] And Wikipedia guidelines specifically provide that "academic and peer-reviewed publications are usually the most reliable sources when available."[32]

Scholarly publications are produced within practices where *Sapere aude* is only half the story.[33] Scholarship requires not only a commitment to vigorous debate and critical freedom, but also and equally a commitment to enforcing standards of judgment and critical rigor.[34] We rely on expert "knowledge" precisely because it has been vetted and reviewed by those whose judgment we have reason to trust. All living disciplines are institutional systems for the production of such "knowledge."

This is explicitly the perspective adopted by federal courts when they determine whether to admit expert testimony about "scientific, technical, or other specialized knowledge" under Federal Rule of Evidence 702.[35] Federal courts plan to rely on such testimony only if it meets "exacting standards of reliability,"[36] which means that an expert's claim to knowledge must be validated by an "assessment of whether the reasoning or methodology underlying the testimony is scientifically valid,"[37] an assessment that in part depends upon "whether the theory or technique has been subjected to peer review and publication."[38]

The continuous discipline of peer judgment, which virtually defines expert knowledge, is quite incompatible with deep and fundamental First Amendment doctrines that impose a "requirement of viewpoint neutrality"[39] on regulations of speech and that apply "the most exacting scrutiny to regulations that suppress, disadvantage, or impose differential burdens upon speech because of its content."[40] If content and viewpoint neutrality is "the cornerstone of the Supreme Court's First Amendment jurisprudence,"[41] the production of expert knowledge rests on quite different foundations. It depends upon the continuous exercise of peer judgment to distinguish meritorious from specious opinions. Expert knowledge requires exactly what normal First Amendment doctrine prohibits. "The First Amendment . . . 'as a general matter . . . means that government has no power to restrict expression because of its message, its ideas, its subject matter, or its content.'"[42]

To put the matter simply, if "the First Amendment recognizes no such thing as a 'false' idea,"[43] then it cannot sustain, or even tolerate, the disciplinary practices necessary to produce expert knowledge. The creation of expert knowledge requires practices that seek to separate true ideas from false ones. A scientific journal bound by First Amendment doctrine, and thus disabled from making necessary editorial judgments about the justification and truth of submissions, could not long survive.[44] Alexander Meiklejohn was quite correct to observe that deep within First Amendment doctrine there is an "equality of status in the field of ideas."[45] This egalitarian commitment is in sharp tension with the cognitive aspiration to knowledge, which in the end must always rely on *discrimination,* in the traditional sense of judgment and evaluation.

It is not intelligible to believe that all *ideas* are equal. Americans repudiate "discrimination," however, because they imagine that *persons,* rather than *ideas,* should be equal. Americans are committed to the equality of persons. The deep egalitarian dimension of the First Amendment resonates far more with this ethical value than with any cognitive ideal. The primary ethical value that has been ascribed to the First Amendment is that of autonomy or individual self-fulfillment, which expresses the principle that all persons ought to be accorded the equal dignity to fulfill their unique individual potential.

I should note at the outset that there is no particular connection between speech and this ethical idea of equal autonomy, because autonomy can be manifested and instantiated through any form of behavior, not merely through communication. There is no doubt that a libertarian commitment to autonomy has deep roots in American constitutionalism and that it has detectably influenced the content of First Amendment doctrine.[46] But the fundamental constitutional commitments of the nation, as reflected in the actual scope of First Amendment coverage, do not suggest that the protection of autonomy can be deemed a basic purpose of the judicially enforced First Amendment.

If the protection of autonomy were a fundamental goal of the First Amendment, all expression equally connected to the achievement of individual self-fulfillment would be accorded equal First Amendment value. But this is emphatically not the case. Much speech that may be of great importance to the autonomy of individual speakers receives no First Amendment coverage at all.

Consider, for example, speech that may be of great importance to a speaker but that is defamatory of another. Well-entrenched First Amendment doctrine holds that if such speech defames a public official or public figure, or if it involves a matter of public concern, the Constitution precludes the application of common law rules that impose liability without fault and that presume damages.[47] The theory is that strict regulation of such speech would be inconsistent with the nation's "profound national commitment" to a robust public debate that will assure the "'unfettered interchange of ideas for the bringing about of political and social changes desired by the people.'"[48] If defamatory speech is about a matter "of purely private concern,"[49] by contrast, "states are free to retain common law principles."[50] First Amendment coverage thus does not extend to private defamatory speech, no matter how important such speech may be to the self-fulfillment of the speaker. First Amendment coverage is extended only when state regulation might adversely affect the value of democratic self-governance.

The same principle of First Amendment coverage applies when the state seeks to regulate the speech of its employees. First Amendment coverage materializes only when employee speech is about a matter "of public concern," because only such speech is "entitled to special protection."[51] First Amendment doctrine attributes no constitutional significance to the importance that such speech may bear to the autonomy or self-fulfillment of an employee.[52] First Amendment coverage is triggered only when a government employee begins "to speak as a citizen addressing matters of public concern."[53] More or less the same standard of First Amendment coverage applies to the tort of intentional infliction of emotional distress[54] and to state efforts to regulate speech in order to protect privacy.[55]

This pervasive and entrenched pattern of First Amendment coverage would make little sense if the protection of autonomy were a fundamental constitutional purpose. Consider a simple case. Many dentists passionately believe that dental amalgams, which are a mixture of silver and mercury used to fill cavities in teeth, are dangerous to the health of their patients because the mercury can leach out and be absorbed by the body.[56] But the American Dental Association and state dental boards consider amalgams safe and appropriate, and they have therefore punished dentists for advising their patients to remove their amalgam fillings. Such advice is thought to expose patients to unnecessary risk and expense. Dentists cannot assert a First Amendment defense to this discipline, just as they generally cannot assert a First Amendment defense to suits for medical malpractice based upon bad advice. It makes no difference how important it may be to the autonomy of an individual dentist to communicate what he believes to be the truth about dental amalgams; it makes no difference how passionately any particular dentist may wish to safeguard the health of his patients.

First Amendment coverage does materialize, however, if a dentist wishes to take her case about dental amalgams to "the general public" by publishing a book or by participating in a television interview.[57] If members of her audience who rely upon her advice and remove their dental amalgams subsequently sue the dentist for "negligent misrepresentation," she may be constitutionally immunized from liability.[58] The autonomy interests of a dentist are the same whether she speaks to the general public in a book or to specific patients in her office, but First Amendment coverage extends to the former and not the latter.[59] This difference cannot be explained by the constitutional value of autonomy. It can be explained only on the hypothesis that speech to the general public is of particular First Amendment importance.

The distinction between public speech and non-public speech is embedded deeply within the fabric of First Amendment doctrine, and it cannot be clarified by autonomy theories of the First Amendment. Communication and conduct that are essential to individual self-definition pervade human society, and the value of autonomy can thus become salient at almost any time and in almost any context. For this reason autonomy theories of the First Amendment have difficulty generating coherent patterns of First Amendment coverage. Whenever we detect such a pattern, and especially when the pattern we detect does not seem sensitive to the concerns of individual autonomy, we must conclude that we are in the presence of a First Amendment purpose that does not express the constitutional value of individual autonomy.

First Amendment coverage does in fact display systematic patterns that are both indifferent to individual autonomy and consistent with the view that the fundamental purpose of the First Amendment is political, rather than ethical. The Court

has time and again explained its own First Amendment jurisprudence in terms of "securing of an informed and educated
public opinion with respect to a matter which is of public
concern."[60]

> The freedom of speech and of the press guaranteed
> by the Constitution embraces at the least the liberty to
> discuss publicly and truthfully all matters of public
> concern without previous restraint or fear of subse-
> quent punishment. . . . Freedom of discussion, if it
> would fulfill its historic function in this nation, must
> embrace all issues about which information is needed
> or appropriate to enable the members of society to
> cope with the exigencies of their period.[61]

The persistent attention in First Amendment doctrine to
whether communication involves *public* officials, or *public* fig-
ures, or matters of *public* concern, or is directed to the general
public, derives from the conviction that, as Learned Hand put
it, "public opinion . . . is the final source of government in a
democratic state."[62] "Public opinion," said James Madison, "is
the real sovereign in every free" government.[63] The function of
the First Amendment is to safeguard the communicative processes by which public opinion is formed, so as to ensure the
integrity of "the great process by which public opinion passes
over into public will, which is legislation."[64] Agreement on
this point is almost universal. Even a thinker like Carl Schmitt
defines democracy as "the rule of public opinion, 'government
by public opinion.'"[65] It is for this reason that we denominate

the antimajoritarian First Amendment the "guardian of our democracy."[66] Even though the very object of the First Amendment is to restrict the laws that a majority may enact, its purpose is to protect the free formation of public opinion that is the sine qua non of democracy.

The contours of First Amendment coverage, the constitutional distinction between speech and action, is therefore to be determined in the first instance by a normative inquiry into the forms of conduct we deem necessary for the free formation of public opinion. Sometimes this conduct occurs through language,[67] and sometimes, as with picketing[67] and flag burning,[68] it does not. First Amendment coverage is "not confined to verbal expression" but "embrace[s] appropriate types of action which certainly include the right in a peaceable and orderly manner to protest by silent and reproachful presence, in a place where the protestant has every right to be."[69] Conversely, vast stretches of ordinary verbal expression, as for example between dentists and their patients, between corporations and their shareholders, between product manufacturers and their customers, are not considered necessary for the formation of public opinion and are consequently excluded from First Amendment coverage.[70] Following the usage of the Court, I shall use the term "public discourse" to refer to the forms of communication constitutionally deemed necessary for formation of public opinion.[71]

Early theorists of the connection between the First Amendment and democracy understood the essence of democracy to lie in the principle of majoritarianism, as expressed through the mechanism of elections.[72] They therefore believed that

First Amendment coverage should extend only to speech that informed voters about matters pertinent to electoral politics. Robert Bork, for example, famously argued that

> [t]he category of protected speech should consist of speech concerned with governmental behavior, policy or personnel. . . . Explicitly political speech is speech about how we are governed, and the category includes a wide range of evaluation, criticism, electioneering and propaganda. It does not cover scientific, education, commercial or literary expressions as such. A novel may have impact upon attitudes that affect politics, but it would not for that reason receive judicial protection. . . . The line drawn must . . . lie between the explicitly political and all else.[73]

Thinking through the implications of this perspective, Alexander Meiklejohn concluded that because the constitutional value of speech lay in informing voters how to exercise the franchise, "What is essential is not that everyone shall speak, but that everything worth saying shall be said."[74] Meiklejohn and Bork believed that First Amendment coverage should not extend to the autonomy interests of speakers, but only to the rights of voters to receive information. Some very great modern scholars of the First Amendment have continued to pursue this framework of analysis.[75]

These conclusions do not correspond to well-entrenched principles of First Amendment coverage, which serve not only "to ensure that the individual citizen can effectively participate in and contribute to our republican system of self-government,"[76] but also to encompass forms of artistic and literary productions that have nothing to do with explicitly political advocacy. "[I]n the area of freedom of speech and press the courts must always remain sensitive to any infringement on genuinely serious literary, artistic, political, or scientific expression."[77]

These disparities between entrenched First Amendment doctrine and the conclusions of early democracy theorists were caused by the fact that the latter possessed a very inadequate understanding of the nature of democracy. They imagined that the basic principle of American democracy was majoritarianism, as expressed through elections. But majoritarianism and elections are merely mechanisms for making decisions. American democracy does not rest upon decision-making techniques, but instead upon the value of self-government, the notion that those who are subject to law should also experience themselves as the authors of law.[78] Constitutional democracy in the United States seeks to instantiate this value by rendering government decisions responsive to public opinion and by guaranteeing to all the possibility of influencing public opinion.

This formulation suggests that judicial First Amendment protections for speech are necessary, although not sufficient, for ensuring democratic legitimacy. If persons are prevented from participating in the formation of public opinion so as to render public opinion responsive to their own point of view, they are not likely to regard themselves as potentially the authors of government decisions that affect them. But it does not follow that they will in fact regard their government as democratically legitimate even if government decisions are responsive to public opinion and even if persons are guaranteed the right to participate in the formation of public opinion. Persons may lack resources to sufficiently participate in the formation of public opinion, or they may have views that are systematically and persistently repudiated by the majority, and so on. The essential point I wish to emphasize, however, is that if persons are prevented even from the possibility of seeking to influence the content of public opinion, there is little hope of democratic legitimation in a modern culturally heterogeneous state.[79] That is why freedom of speech is generally the first and most pressing demand in any state experiencing a transition to democracy.

II.

It follows from this analysis that First Amendment coverage should extend to all efforts deemed normatively necessary for influencing public opinion. We know that public opinion is formed within what sociologists call the "public sphere," and we know that historically "the public sphere in the political realm evolved from the public sphere in the world of letters."[80] Following the development of affordable and widely dispersed printed material, like books and newspapers, the public sphere became an arena in which strangers could communicate systematically and regularly with each other. This is the precondition for the very idea of a "public opinion."

The development of the public sphere was a fundamental "mutation" in the development of the modern "social imaginary."[81] It enabled "members of society" for the first time to envision themselves as engaging each other "through a variety of media: print and electronic as well as face-to-face encounters, wherein they discuss matters of common interest and thus are able to form a common mind about these."[82] The concept of a "public" emerges from "the circulation of texts among strangers who become, by virtue of their reflexively circulating discourse, a social entity."[83] The public sphere can sustain democratic legitimation only insofar as it is beyond the grasp of comprehensive state managerial control:

> If it were not possible to think of the public as organized independently of the state . . . , the public could not be sovereign with respect to the state. . . . The peculiar character of *a* public is that it is a space of discourse organized by discourse. It is self-creating and self-organized; and herein lies its power, as well as its elusive strangeness. . . . Speaking, writing, and thinking involve us—actively and immediately—in a public, and thus in the being of the sovereign.[84]

Democracy requires that government action be tethered to public opinion. Because public opinion can direct government action in an endless variety of directions, it is impossible to specify in advance which aspects of public opinion are "political" and which are not. A novel like *The Jungle* might inspire the reform of government inspection procedures for food; a movie like *Missing* might encourage a re-examination of foreign policy; the sad tale of Charlie Sheen might instigate a re-examination of public health policies toward the mentally disturbed, and so on. It is for this reason that First Amendment coverage presumptively extends to all communications that form public opinion. Most especially, First Amendment coverage presumptively extends to media for the communication of ideas, like newspapers, magazines, the Internet, or cinema, which are the primary vehicles for the circulation of the texts that define and sustain the public sphere.[85] In the absence of strong countervailing reasons, whatever is said within such media is covered by the First Amendment.

Because we think of public opinion as "sovereign" in a democracy, we tend to imagine public opinion as agential, as deciding questions like war or price regulation or universal health insurance.[86] This tendency is reinforced by the irrepressible desire of political scientists and pollsters to measure the "content" of public opinion, to inform us whether the median voter approves or disapproves of financial bailouts or Guantánamo detentions or estate taxes. For First Amendment purposes, however, public opinion is not conceived in this agential way. The Constitution instead regards public opinion as continuously evolving within the public sphere. Democracy does not require that government be subordinated to any particular temporary manifestation of public opinion. It requires rather that public opinion remain continuously open to revision.

Democratic nations deploy a variety of mechanisms to subordinate governmental decision-making to public opinion. Elections are the most obvious and pervasive such mechanism. There are many ways to construct elections, but even the best-designed election can at most reflect the content of public opinion at a particular moment in time. The larger perspective of the First Amendment is not so blinkered; it regards public opinion as perpetually in motion. From the constitutional point of view, therefore, public opinion is a verb rather than a noun. Public opinion does not possess the internal consistency or integrity that is characteristic of agents who must decide and act. It is instead transactional and subjectless. The object of the First Amendment might most precisely be characterized as protecting the open processes by which public opinion is constantly formed and reformed.

Like any form of government, a democracy must make decisions, even irretrievable ones, and it must act on these decisions with consistency and integrity. But democracy is unique because it embeds state decision-making within communicative processes that continuously reconsider and reevaluate official decisions. Even as a democratic state carries out the decisions of its government, therefore, it must remain ultimately accountable to potentially kaleidoscopic communicative processes. Habermas is thus rigorously accurate to conclude that in a democracy "sovereignty is found" in "subjectless forms of communication that regulate the flow of discursive opinion- and will-formation," so that "popular sovereignty withdraws into democratic procedures and the demanding communicative presuppositions of their implementation."[87]

Within public discourse, the First Amendment protects the autonomy of speakers, not merely the rights of audiences. If persons within public discourse are prevented from choosing what to communicate or not to communicate, the value of democratic legitimation will not be served. Persons will not experience participation in public discourse as a means of making government responsive to their own personal views. That is why the First Amendment has been interpreted to prohibit the state from compelling persons to speak within public discourse, even to the extent of mandating that persons disclose true and material facts. "There is certainly some difference between compelled speech and compelled silence, but in the context of protected speech, the difference is without constitutional significance, for the First Amendment guarantees 'freedom of speech,' a term necessarily comprising the decision of both what to say and what not to say."[88] "Mandating speech that a speaker would not otherwise make necessarily alters the content of the speech,"[89] but "[t]he First Amendment mandates that we presume that speakers, not the government, know best both what they want to say and how to say it."[90] The government cannot require that the *New York Times* publish information deemed by the government necessary for a complete understanding of a breaking news story.

At root, First Amendment prohibitions against viewpoint and content discrimination express the essential postulate that all persons within public discourse should be equally free to say or not say what they choose. This equality reflects the premise that in a democracy every subject of law possesses an equal right to seek to shape the content of public opinion and so to influence government action. Those bound by law are entitled to the imaginative possibility that public opinion will be responsive to their views; this possibility underwrites their capacity to experience the state as democratically legitimate.

Government regulations of speech are very different outside the sphere of public discourse. Government routinely requires persons to speak,[91] whether it compels manufacturers to label their products or doctors to report patients with AIDS or motorists to report accidents. It routinely engages in content and viewpoint discrimination, managing speech based upon its substance, whether through the law of professional malpractice or commercial misrepresentation or securities regulation. Whereas within public discourse the political imperatives of democracy require that persons be regarded as equal and as autonomous,[92] outside public discourse the law commonly regards persons as dependent, vulnerable, and hence unequal.[93] Clients are legally entitled to rely on the advice of their lawyers; consumers on the representations of manufacturers; shareholders on the information of corporations. That is why law holds lawyers accountable for malpractice, manufacturers for the failure to warn, and corporations for misrepresentation. Within public discourse, by contrast, the First Amendment ascribes autonomy equally to speakers and to their audience, so that the rule of caveat emptor applies. A member of the general public who foolishly removes his silver fillings upon reading a dentist's book is held responsible for his own bad decision.[94]

This contrast is quite stark, and it is the single most salient pattern of entrenched First Amendment doctrine. The contrast suggests one further reason why interpreting the First Amendment to serve the value of autonomy would be undesirable. There are times when we wish law to ascribe to persons the virtue of autonomy, and there are times when we wish law to ascribe to persons the vulnerability of dependence. In actual social life, of course, persons are always *both* autonomous and dependent. The question is how we wish the law ascriptively to regard them.[95] If the First Amendment were to require the state to regard all communication through the lens of autonomy, it would disable law from making this important distinction.

The point is especially important when government seeks to enforce dimensions of communicative respect that define the dignity and self-worth of persons.[96] I refer here to the law of libel, privacy, outrageous infliction of emotional distress, hate speech, and so on. The enforcement of such laws is essential for healthy human development, and yet the ascribed assumption of autonomy precludes the enforcement of these laws within the sphere of public discourse. Racist speech can be punished in secondary schools and in the workplace, but not in the *New York Times*. Within public discourse, the First Amendment requires law to respect the autonomy of speakers rather than to protect the targets of speech; outside public discourse, the First Amendment permits the state to control the autonomy of speakers in order to protect the dignity of the targets of speech. I do not think that an autonomy view of the First Amendment can explain or accept this distinction.

A democratic interpretation of the First Amendment, by contrast, possesses the capacity to adjust the boundary between public discourse and non-public discourse in ways that allow law to designate when autonomy should and should not be legally ascribed.[97] It can formulate judicially enforced rights so as to incorporate the sociological insight that some such boundary is necessary if a society is to entrench the civility norms necessary for social cohesion and identity. Almost all democratic accounts of the First Amendment seek to differentiate a political domain of public opinion creation from non-political domains of civil society. This distinction would be merely arbitrary if the First Amendment were understood as ascribing the value of autonomy to the speech of all persons.

If the central thrust of the First Amendment is democratic legitimation, and if this value precludes content discrimination, we can begin to appreciate the full depth of the puzzle with which I began this chapter. It would at first glance appear that wherever First Amendment doctrine applies, it suppresses legal support for the disciplinary practices necessary for endowing beliefs with the reliability that defines disciplinary knowledge. "To call a field a 'discipline,'" after all, "is to suggest that . . . its authority does not derive from the writings of an individual or a school, but rather from generally accepted methods and truths."[98] "Any institutionalized method for producing knowledge has its foundations in social conventions: conventions concerning how the knowledge is to be produced, about what may be questioned and what may not, about what is normally expected and what counts as an anomaly, about what is to be regarded as evidence and proof."[99] Disciplinary knowledge cannot be produced without such conventions, methods, and truths.[100] Yet First Amendment doctrine serves the value of democratic legitimation by preventing government from imposing any such conventions, methods, and truths within public discourse.

How then should we conceive the relationship between the First Amendment and the production and dissemination of expert knowledge? It is to that question that I turn in Chapter Two.

2

Democratic Competence and the First Amendment

The First Amendment guarantees the free formation of public opinion. But public opinion is, in the end, merely opinion. Hegel recognized this early on:

> The formal subjective freedom of individuals consists in their having and expressing their own private judgements, opinions, and recommendations on affairs of state. This freedom is collectively manifested as what is called "public opinion," in which what is absolutely universal, the substantive and the true, is linked with its opposite, the purely particular and private opinions of the Many.[1]

It is precisely because public opinion reflects the subjective perspective of individuals that the First Amendment prohibits the state from denying persons access to public discourse. The goal of democratic legitimation is a primary purpose of the First Amendment, and the possibility of democratic legitimation lies in the hope that persons who are permitted the opportunity to make public opinion responsive to their own subjective, personal views might come to regard themselves as the potential authors of the laws that bind them.

If public opinion is merely *opinion*, then it lacks the indicia of reliability that define knowledge. As Hegel immediately saw, public opinion "in itself . . . has no criterion of discrimination, nor has it the ability to extract the substantive element it contains and raise it to precise knowledge. Thus to be independent of public opinion is the first formal condition of achieving anything great or rational whether in life or in science."[2] By the middle of the nineteenth century this tension between public opinion and knowledge was so great that John Stuart Mill could recognize that "[t]he modern *regime* of public opinion is, in an unorganized form, what the Chinese educational and political systems are in an organized; and unless individuality shall be able successfully to assert itself against this yoke, Europe, notwithstanding its noble antecedents and its professed Christianity, will tend to become another China."[3] Mill felt the need for protection "against the tyranny of the prevailing opinion and feeling, against the tendency of society to impose, by other means than civil penalties, its own ideas and practices as rules of conduct on those who dissent from them."[4]

The fundamental First Amendment doctrine of content neutrality is meant to prevent the state from cutting persons off from access to processes of public opinion formation on the basis of what they intend to say. The doctrine advances the goal of democratic legitimation by ensuring that public opinion remains open to the subjective engagement of all, even of the idiosyncratic and eccentric. Fools and savants are equally entitled to address the public.

What we characterize as expert knowledge, by contrast, is not to be determined by the indiscriminate engagement of all. Technical beliefs do not become reliable merely because they are widely shared. As Thomas Kuhn has observed, "One of the strongest, if still unwritten, rules of scientific life is the prohibition of appeals to heads of state or to the populace at large in matters scientific."[5] We regard scientific beliefs as reliable because they are subject to disciplinary standards of verifiability, reproducibility, falsifiability, and so on.[6] These standards cannot constitutionally be enforced within public discourse. The state can enforce them only within some venue outside of public discourse in which the need for producing reliable knowledge subordinates the egalitarian principle of democratic legitimation.

An important qualification to this conclusion concerns factual truth. "Freedom of opinion," Hannah Arendt writes, "is a farce unless factual information is guaranteed and the facts themselves are not in dispute. . . . [F]actual truth informs political thought."[7] Entrenched First Amendment doctrine affirms that "there is no constitutional value in false statements of fact."[8] Thus even as courts hold that "under the First Amendment there is no such thing as a false idea,"[9] they also permit the state to regulate the publication of false facts, even within public discourse.

The difficulty is that government control over factual truth is in tension with the value of democratic legitimation. Citizens who seek to participate in public discourse, and who are penalized because they disagree with official versions of factual truth, are excluded from the possibility of influencing public opinion.[10] Although we might postulate a world in which reasonable persons do not disagree about factual truth, we all know that as a practical matter this is not the case. Intense and consequential disputes about factual questions abound. Insofar as the state intervenes definitively to settle these disputes, it alienates persons from participation in public discourse.

First Amendment jurisprudence tends to negotiate this tension through doctrines like that of "actual malice"[11] or "fault,"[12] which prohibit the state from punishing citizens for mere factual error. These doctrines prevent the state from punishing citizens participating in public discourse simply because they have made a factual mistake. The state can punish such citizens only if it shows that they also have some guilty state of mind, like negligence or the deliberate intent to mislead. Doctrines requiring this special form of mens rea are designed to create a "breathing space" that immunizes participants in public discourse from the fear that they might be punished for innocent factual mistakes.[13]

In matters of expert knowledge, courts use additional techniques to maintain the openness of public discourse. Entrenched First Amendment doctrine holds that although the state may penalize false assertions of fact, it may not regulate false assertions of opinion. Courts construe this distinction in a manner that errs "on the side of nonactionability."[14] Statements "that describe present or past conditions capable of being known through sense impressions"[15] are classified as factual, whereas statements in which a speaker "is expressing a subjective view, an interpretation, a theory, conjecture, or surmise"[16] tend to be classified as protected opinion.

Because courts view "scientific truth [as] elusive" and believe that "scientific controversies must be settled by the methods of science rather than by the methods of litigation,"[17] they characteristically regard expert judgments as nonactionable ideas. "More papers, more discussion, better data, and more satisfactory models—not larger awards of damages—mark the path toward superior understanding of the world around us."[18] Courts self-consciously "foster a public forum for the robust debate that identifies scientific truths."[19] The upshot is that within public discourse courts are reluctant to use law to enforce the disciplinary standards that define expert knowledge. Even about matters that are squarely within the competence of recognized disciplines, there are no preconditions or qualifications for participation in the formation of public opinion.

"In the world of opinion," Michael Walzer writes, "truth is indeed another opinion."[20] The value of democratic legitimation causes First Amendment doctrine to construct public discourse as a domain of opinion because it prevents the state from maintaining the standards of reliability that we associate with expert knowledge. Within public discourse, the message of the First Amendment is *caveat emptor*. The creation of reliable disciplinary knowledge must accordingly be relegated to institutions that are not controlled by the constitutional value of democratic legitimation.

This division of labor has been theorized by Allen Buchanan, who argues for the necessity of "key liberal institutions" capable of authorizing "a comparatively large role for merit in the social identification of reliable sources of belief (epistemic authorities), where 'merit' means the possession of objective qualifications rationally related to the functions of particular social roles and positions."[21] Buchanan notes that "among the most important social institutions for the production of true beliefs are (1) the social division of labor and (2) the social identification of experts, that is, epistemic authorities, individuals or groups to whom others defer as reliable sources of true beliefs."[22] The "unrestrained epistemic egalitarianism" imposed by the First Amendment on public discourse is incompatible with "the division of epistemic labor" necessary for the production of expert knowledge.[23]

There are good reasons to support liberal institutions of the kind described by Buchanan. No less a democrat than John Dewey has recognized that "opinions and beliefs concerning the public presuppose effective and organized inquiry" and that "genuine public policy cannot be generated unless it be informed by knowledge, and this knowledge does not exist except when there is systematic, thorough, and well-equipped search and record."[24] Expert knowledge is prerequisite for intelligent self-governance.

Recall in this context the grim regime of Trofim D. Lysenko, who prohibited Soviet biologists from investigating genetics on the ground that Marxism required all forms of behavior to be explained by environmental influences.[25] Lysenko's efforts to impose political control over the epistemological structure of Soviet science inflicted long-standing damage on the development of Soviet biology. On the other side of the spectrum, we recently witnessed an assault on expert knowledge by members of the Bush administration who believed that their political mandate authorized them to reject the "judicious study of discernible reality" and instead to create "our own reality."[26]

Reliable expert knowledge is necessary not only for intelligent self-governance, but also for the very value of democratic legitimation. As the eminent French political theorist Claude Lefort has argued, democratic states are distinguishable from totalitarian regimes because in the latter

> a condensation takes place between the sphere of power, the sphere of law and the sphere of knowledge. Knowledge of the ultimate goals of society and of the norms which regulate social practices becomes the property of power, and at the same time power itself claims to be the organ of discourse which articulates the real as such.[27]

A state that controls our knowledge controls our minds.[28] Because "contemporary Western societies are in one sense or another ruled by knowledge and expertise,"[29] a state that can manipulate the production of disciplinary knowledge can set the terms of its own legitimacy. It can undermine the capacity of citizens to form autonomous and critical opinions.[30] It can make a mockery of the obligation of democratic government to be responsive to the views of its citizens.

There are thus good reasons to ensure that the production of disciplinary knowledge remain at least partially independent from state control. It is one thing to identify a social need, however, and it is quite another to identify a set of constitutional principles that serve to address that need. My question in this chapter is whether we can discern distinct First Amendment doctrines designed to protect the social practices that produce and distribute disciplinary knowledge. These principles would serve a constitutional value that I shall call "democratic competence." Democratic competence refers to the cognitive empowerment of persons within public discourse, which in part depends on their access to disciplinary knowledge. Cognitive empowerment is necessary both for intelligent self-governance and for the value of democratic legitimation.

To theorize the value of democratic competence is to confront a seeming paradox. Democratic *legitimation* requires that the speech of all persons be treated with toleration and equality. Democratic *competence,* by contrast, requires that speech be subject to a disciplinary authority that distinguishes good ideas from bad ones. Yet democratic competence is necessary for democratic legitimation. Democratic competence is thus both incompatible with democratic legitimation and required by it. This is an awkward conclusion that should prompt us to think hard about how democratic competence can be reconciled with democratic legitimation.

It is plain that within public discourse the value of democratic legitimation enjoys lexical priority. Democratic identity and will is forged within public discourse, and nothing is more fundamental for democracy. But there are many forms of communication that lie outside public discourse and that are not governed by its constitutional requirements. Judicial doctrine that serves the distinct value of democratic competence is likely to be most identifiable in these spheres of non-public discourse. In this chapter, I explore whether we can recognize judicial decisions that require state regulation of such spheres to respect, and perhaps even to maintain, the value of democratic competence.

One relevant line of precedent concerns contemporary commercial speech doctrine, which vigorously protects the dissemination of factual information outside of public discourse. Oddly enough, commercial speech doctrine is best explained as resting on the constitutional value of democratic competence. There are also scattered court decisions that serve this same value by protecting the distribution of disciplinary knowledge outside of public discourse. These decisions are rare and fragmentary, but they are nevertheless intuitively robust. They yield the unexpected conclusion that our First Amendment has been interpreted to shield from unchecked political control the authoritative disciplinary practices that produce expert knowledge.

I.

Democracy subordinates government to public opinion. It follows that an educated and informed public opinion will more intelligently and effectively supervise the government. Bentham noticed early on that "[i]n an assembly elected by the people, and renewed from time to time, publicity is absolutely necessary to enable the electors to act from knowledge."[31] Madison made a similar observation: "A popular Government, without popular information, or the means of acquiring it, is but a Prologue to a Farce or a Tragedy."[32]

The entire theory of the First Amendment espoused by Meiklejohn developed from this basic point. He argued that freedom of speech was necessary in order to ensure

the voting of wise decisions. . . . The welfare of the community requires that those who decide issues shall understand them. . . . Just so far as, at any point,

the citizens who are to decide an issue are denied ac-
quaintance with information or opinion, or doubt or
disbelief or criticism which is relevant to that issue,
just so far the result must be ill-considered, ill-balanced
planning for the general good. *It is that mutilation of
the thinking process of the community against which
the First Amendment of the Constitution is directed.*[33]

This approach to the First Amendment does not con-
ceptualize its primary purpose to be establishing democratic
legitimacy, but rather facilitating democratic competence. It
understands the function of public communication to be edu-
cating the electorate, and hence, as Meiklejohn clearly saw, it
affirms that the First Amendment must take as its "point of
ultimate interest . . . not the words of the speakers, but the
minds of the hearers."[34] Meiklejohn was explicit that the First
Amendment "does not require that, on every occasion, every
citizen shall take part in public debate. Nor can it even give
assurance that everyone shall have opportunity to do so. . . .
What is essential is not that everyone shall speak, but that
everything worth saying shall be said."[35]

We know that Meiklejohn's approach does not describe
the First Amendment as it applies to public discourse, because
entrenched First Amendment doctrine does indeed guarantee
the right of every citizen to take part in public debate.[36] To
exclude any person from public discourse is to deny that person the possibility of using speech to make public opinion responsive to his views, and hence to deny him the possibility of
striving for democratic legitimation. Within public discourse

the value of democratic legitimation trumps that of democratic competence.

It does not follow, however, that democratic competence drops out of the picture altogether. In those rare cases when the right of a speaker to communicate and the right of an audience to receive information are not perfectly symmetrical, the Court has not hesitated to defend the independent right of an audience to receive information willingly communicated.[37] And there have also been cases in which the Court has held that "the right to attend criminal trials is implicit in the guarantees of the First Amendment," because "the explicit, guaranteed rights to speak and to publish concerning what takes place at a trial would lose much meaning if access to observe the trial could . . . be foreclosed arbitrarily."[38]

Outside the context of court proceedings that have traditionally been open to the public, however, the Court has been exceedingly reluctant to interpret the First Amendment to require government disclosure of information to enhance democratic competence. It has regarded the job of deciding which government information to disclose and which to withhold as "clearly a legislative task which the Constitution has left to the political processes."[39]

There is no discernible basis for a constitutional duty to disclose, or for standards governing disclosure of or access to information. Because the Constitution affords no guidelines, absent statutory standards, hundreds of judges would, under the Court of Appeals' approach, be at large to fashion ad hoc standards, in individual cases, according to their own ideas of what seems "desirable" or expedient." . . .

> "There is no constitutional right to have access to particular government information, or to require openness from the bureaucracy. . . . The public's interest in knowing about its government is protected by the guarantee of a Free Press, but the protection is indirect. The Constitution itself is neither a Freedom of Information Act nor an Official Secrets Act."[40]

This allocation of authority to fulfill a potential constitutional value is best interpreted either as evidence of the Court's commitment to legislative constitutionalism, or as expressing a deep, analytically obscure[41] distinction between affirmative and negative rights.[42] American courts are far more comfortable preventing government from regulating individuals than they are requiring government to act at the behest of individuals. If we are to find robust evidence of judicial enforcement of the value of democratic competence, it will most likely involve negative rights that prohibit government from regulating individuals who wish to disseminate information or knowledge outside of public discourse.

There is in fact well-developed judicial doctrine to this effect. I am referring to commercial speech doctrine. In the 1970s, the United States Supreme Court repudiated its longstanding conclusion that "the Constitution imposes no . . . restraint on government" regulation of "purely commercial advertising."[43] Commercial advertising had been unprotected because it was outside public discourse. Everyone understood that seeking to sell toothpaste was a different kind of communicative act than attempting to influence the content of public opinion. But in 1976 the Court held that First Amendment coverage should extend to commercial advertising:

> Advertising . . . is nonetheless dissemination of information as to who is producing and selling what product, for what reason, and at what price. So long as we preserve a predominantly free enterprise economy, the allocation of our resources in large measure will be made through numerous private economic decisions. It is a matter of public interest that those decisions, in the aggregate, be intelligent and well informed. To this end, the free flow of commercial information is indispensable. . . . And if it is indispensable to the proper allocation of resources in a free enterprise system, it is also indispensable to the formation of intelligent opinions as to how that system ought to be regulated or altered. Therefore, even if the First Amendment were thought to be primarily an instrument to enlighten public decision-making in a democracy, we could not say that the free flow of information does not serve that goal.[44]

The passage seems to offer two distinct reasons for extending First Amendment coverage to commercial advertising. The first is that advertising is necessary for the efficient functioning of commercial markets. On this account, market efficiency is an independent constitutional value, and advertising receives constitutional protection in order to protect market efficiency. But this reasoning is unconvincing. The First Amendment serves the value of democratic legitimation by protecting the communicative processes through which the public decides whether to pursue the goal of market efficiency or whether to subordinate that goal to other objectives like redistribution or paternalism. To attribute independent constitutional value to market efficiency is to restrict legislative choices in the name, as Oliver Wendell Holmes famously said in his dissent in *Lochner v. New York*, of the particular socioeconomic vision advanced in "Mr. Herbert Spencer's *Social Statics.*"[45] Any such interpretation of the First Amendment would contradict the fundamental value of democratic legitimation, which invests public opinion with the authority (within broad limits) to decide what forms of market management should be endorsed by the state.

The second reason advanced by the Court for extending First Amendment coverage to commercial advertising suffers from no such fatal liability. The Court states that commercial advertising should be covered by the First Amendment because it is relevant to "public decision-making in a democracy." Advertising conveys information pertinent "to the formation of intelligent opinions as to how" the American economy should be regulated. "Advertising, though entirely commercial, may often carry information of import to significant issues of the day,"[46] and for this reason deserves constitutional protection in order to safeguard "the essential role that the free flow of information plays in a democratic society."[47]

To assert that First Amendment coverage should extend to commercial advertising because it conveys factual knowledge that cognitively empowers public opinion is to affirm that speech can be protected because it serves the value of democratic competence. It is not surprising, therefore, that the shape of commercial speech doctrine follows roughly Meiklejohnian lines, as indeed does the First Amendment doctrine applied to state regulations seeking to control the circulation of non-advertising commercial information outside of public discourse.[48] The Court has explained that "[t]he First Amendment's concern for commercial speech is based on the informational function of advertising,"[49] and therefore that "the extension of First Amendment protection to commercial speech is justified principally by the value to consumers of the information such speech provides."[50] "A commercial advertisement is constitutionally protected not so much because it pertains to the seller's business as because it furthers the societal interest in the 'free flow of commercial information.'"[51]

Important doctrinal consequences follow from these constitutional premises. Because the constitutional value of commercial speech lies in the information that it carries, the state can engage in content discrimination to regulate and suppress the circulation of "misleading" information.[52] The contrast to permissible regulations of public discourse is stark.[53] It would be forbidden content discrimination for the state to suppress "misleading" speech within public discourse. Such suppression would be inconsistent with the equal right of every speaker to participate in the formation of public opinion. But "'the First Amendment . . . does not prohibit the State from insuring that the stream of commercial information flow[s] cleanly as well as freely.'"[54] Government regularly scrutinizes the content of commercial speech[55] to insure that it conveys reliable, rather than misleading, information. Only in this way can the value of democratic competence be served.

Commercial speakers are commonly compelled to speak in ways that enhance the information they circulate.[56] To augment the efficiency and transparency of markets, the state routinely requires commercial speakers to divulge information about products they sell. If applied to public discourse, such compulsion would transgress the subjective experience of speakers who seek to shape public opinion to reflect their own personal perspectives about matters they regard as important. That is why the First Amendment prohibits the state from compelling political commentators to be accurate, fair, and balanced.[57] Such compulsion risks alienating speakers from their own communication.[58] It thus undermines democratic legitimation. But because commercial speech is not protected in order to promote democratic legitimation, but instead to serve democratic competence, it is constitutionally permissible to compel commercial speech. Such compulsion can augment the flow of accurate information to the public and so actually advance the constitutional purpose of public education.[59]

We can learn important lessons from commercial speech doctrine. It demonstrates that entrenched First Amendment standards do indeed protect the flow of information so as to enhance the quality of public decision-making. These standards are oriented to the rights of audiences to receive information rather than to the rights of speakers to communicate. They thus display properties that are inconsistent with the First Amendment rules that govern public discourse. Commercial speech doctrine authorizes the state to engage in content discrimination to suppress misleading information, and it empowers the state to compel the disclosure of information. The structure of commercial speech doctrine is in these respects antithetical to First Amendment protections for public discourse.

II.

If the circulation of commercial information serves the value of democratic competence, so also does the circulation of expert knowledge. Constitutional protections for the dissemination of expert knowledge should therefore be roughly analogous to those applicable to the circulation of commercial information. Important distinctions between commercial information and disciplinary knowledge, however, introduce significant variations in constitutional doctrine.

Unlike commercial information, expert knowledge is not the object of a distinct and well-recognized branch of First Amendment jurisprudence. If we wish to make visible our existing constitutional instincts in this area, we must scrutinize domains outside of public discourse. This is because communication of expert knowledge within public discourse is typically protected by the value of democratic legitimation, which can obscure the distinct protections inspired by democratic competence. If an expert chooses to participate in public discourse by speaking about matters within her expertise, her speech will characteristically be classified as fully protected opinion. That is why the dentist I described in Chapter One who addressed the general public about the dangers of dental amalgams received First Amendment immunity.

Constitutional protections for disciplinary speech within public discourse preclude the state from holding expert speech to ordinary standards of disciplinary competence. The state cannot enforce the disciplinary methods that make expert knowledge reliable. The value of democratic legitimation protects the interests of speakers who wish to participate in the formation of public opinion rather than the interests of audience members who wish to rely on the truth of speech. Biologists can with impunity write editorials in the *New York Times* that are such poor science that they would constitute grounds for denying tenure within a university. Members of the general public can rely on expert pronouncements within public discourse only at their peril.[60] Such pronouncements are ultimately subject to political rather than legal accountability. The "traditional authority" that might otherwise attach to "expertise" is thus constitutionally undermined and rendered vulnerable to "dialogic engagement."[61] Some, like Anthony Giddens, regard this as a cause for celebration. Within public discourse, traditional First Amendment doctrine systematically transmutes claims of expert knowledge into assertions of opinion.

Outside of public discourse, by contrast, the First Amendment functions quite differently. Just as commercial speech doctrine authorizes content discrimination to ensure that commercial information is not misleading, so malpractice law outside of public discourse rigorously polices the authority of disciplinary knowledge. It underwrites the competence of experts. Doctors, dentists, lawyers, or architects who offer what authoritative professional standards would regard as incompetent advice to their clients face strict legal regulation. In such contexts, law stands as a surety for the disciplinary truth of expert pronouncements. By guaranteeing that clients can plan to rely on expert professional judgment, law endows such communication with the status of knowledge.

Malpractice liability attaches equally to incompetent advice and to the failure to offer advice that ought to be provided.[62] In this sense malpractice law compels communication. It requires professionals to speak. As in the context of commercial speech doctrine, law regulating the circulation of expert knowledge outside of public discourse adopts an audience perspective in order to preserve the integrity of communication.

A striking peculiarity of established constitutional doctrine is that First Amendment coverage does not typically extend to malpractice litigation. A doctor who offers bad advice to a patient cannot defend a consequent tort suit on the ground that his opinion was constitutionally immunized from liability. He cannot claim that his advice was an experiment, as all life is an experiment. A lawyer who serves up an incompetent legal opinion cannot defend a subsequent malpractice suit on the ground that the law must respect his individual autonomy or on the ground that the law must protect the marketplace of ideas. The law will simply ask whether the lawyer's opinion did or did not meet relevant professional standards of competence. If a patient relies to her detriment on the advice of a dentist who commits what the American Dental Association considers malpractice and advises the removal of silver fillings, the First Amendment will not serve as a defense in the subsequent malpractice action.

This poses something of a puzzle. Why should First Amendment coverage extend to the circulation of commercial information outside of public discourse, but not to the circulation of expert knowledge? One distinction that might immediately strike us is that commercial speech tends to be addressed to the general public in advertisements that are placed in newspapers or radio or other media that are widely distributed. The information contained in commercial speech thus tends to have an obvious impact on public opinion. The advice offered by an expert professional, by contrast, is typically given only to a single person. It is not broadcast to the public sphere, and so its potential effect on public opinion is far less apparent.

This distinction does not seem to me decisive, because there is no reason why public opinion might not be formed one conversation at a time. If a person learns through the advice of their dentist that dental amalgams are dangerous, they might wish to support legislation regulating the availability of such treatments. There are certainly groups who presently advocate for such reform.[63] So long as knowledge is potentially relevant to the formation of public opinion, I do not see in principle why it should constitutionally matter whether it is distributed to one person or to a thousand.

The difference between commercial speech and expert knowledge seems to me a matter of quality rather than quantity. Commercial speech doctrine covers commercial advertisements typically addressed to an audience that is mature, independent, and free to accept or reject their blandishments. The doctrine *presupposes* equality between an advertiser and its audience, and indeed the Court has refused to apply First Amendment coverage when this equality is lacking.[64] Yet this equality is specifically and emphatically absent in the case of professional clientele.

In law and in social practice clients are *entitled* to rely on the truth and accuracy of a professional's judgment. Clients are presumed to be dependent upon professional judgment and unable themselves independently to evaluate its quality. If the extension of First Amendment coverage to the circulation of commercial information presupposes that persons can reach their own conclusions based upon commercial information, the refusal to extend First Amendment coverage to professional malpractice litigation suggests the opposite premise, that clients cannot second-guess the expert knowledge of professionals. Malpractice law protects the vulnerability of clients by requiring professionals to maintain strict standards of expert knowledge.

Seen from this perspective, the very absence of First Amendment coverage from the context of malpractice litigation emphasizes the *significance* which law attributes to the circulation of accurate expert knowledge. This significance implies that First Amendment coverage might arise in contexts that are distinct from malpractice, in which the state may seek to corrupt, rather than to protect, the diffusion of expert knowledge.

Consider, for example, legislation which *prohibits* expert professionals from communicating knowledge to their clients, or, conversely, legislation which *compels* professionals to communicate false information to their clients.[65] Such legislation is the opposite of malpractice law, which guarantees the circulation of competent expert knowledge. If the value of democratic competence attaches to the communication of expert knowledge, as it does to the communication of commercial information, we should expect to see First Amendment coverage triggered whenever government seeks by such legislation to disrupt the communication of accurate expert knowledge.[66]

First Amendment coverage is in fact visible in such circumstances. In a recent decision, for example, a Nebraska statute forcing doctors "to give untruthful, misleading and irrelevant information to patients" was held to implicate the "First Amendment rights of medical providers" and was accordingly enjoined.[67] Or consider § 526 (a)(4) of the Bankruptcy Abuse Prevention and Consumer Protection Act of 2005 ("BAPCPA"),[68] which provides that

(a) A debt relief agency shall not . . .

(4) advise an assisted person or prospective assisted person to incur more debt in contemplation of such person filing a case under this title or to pay an attorney or bankruptcy petition preparer fee or charge for services performed as part of preparing for or representing a debtor in a case under this title.

When lower courts first encountered this statutory provision, some were so concerned to avoid "grave constitutional questions" that they refused to interpret the term "debt relief agency" to apply to bankruptcy lawyers.[69] Other courts, unable to stretch the statute quite so far, concluded that attorneys were indeed subject to the prohibition of BAPCPA.[70] Such courts were brought face to face with a statute they believed prohibited attorneys from communicating truthful and relevant legal knowledge to their clients. These courts believed that BAPCPA prevented lawyers from advising clients that they could incur debt in contemplation of bankruptcy, which in fact clients were legally entitled to do.

BAPCPA prohibits transmission of this knowledge because it fears that potential bankrupts might "improperly" enlarge "pre-existing debt, thereby diluting the assets of the bankruptcy estate otherwise available to creditors."[71] There are, however, rational and honorable reasons for incurring debt in contemplation of bankruptcy. "[L]egitimate incursions of debt could be the refinance of a mortgage that allows a debtor to pay off the mortgage and other debts, such as credit card debt, in a chapter 13 where failure to refinance may only allow the debtor sufficient funds to pay off one or the other but not both."[72] Federal courts thus understood BAPCPA to prohibit "attorneys, in certain instances, from giving the best and most complete advice to their clients."[73] Because Congress's reasons for prohibiting this advice were outweighed by the need to communicate accurate legal advice serving legal and honorable purposes, every lower federal court to have considered the question found § 526(a)(4) to be unconstitutional under the First Amendment.[74]

The Supreme Court ultimately decided the constitutionality of BAPCPA in March 2010. The Justices unanimously concluded that although § 526(a)(4) applied to attorneys, it prohibited only legal advice that encouraged "a specific type of misconduct designed to manipulate the protections of the bankruptcy system"—the incurring of "more debt because the debtor is filing for bankruptcy, rather than for a valid purpose."[75] Incurring debt for this reason constitutes "conduct that is abusive *per se.*"[76] The Court reasoned that "it is hard to see how a rule that narrowly prohibits an attorney from affirmatively advising a client to commit this type of abusive prefiling conduct could chill attorney speech or inhibit the attorney-client relationship."[77]

The Supreme Court took great care to read § 526(a)(4) in a manner that would avoid the constitutional questions that had troubled lower courts. The Court refused to construe the statute to prevent attorneys from providing clients accurate legal knowledge about legal rights. Instead the Court twisted the statute to mean that attorneys could not affirmatively advise clients to abuse the legal system.[78] Interpreted in this narrow fashion, the statute does no more than to enforce ethical obligations that the legal profession imposes upon itself.[79]

It is fair to conclude that every federal court to have considered § 526(a)(4) appreciated that First Amendment coverage would extend to a statute that forbids lawyers from disclosing to clients, in the privacy of the attorney-client relationship, knowledge about the nature of their legal rights. If ordinary malpractice suits routinely regulate such attorney speech (and non-speech) without any First Amendment coverage,[80] why would such coverage suddenly arise in the context of a statute like § 526(a)(4)?

I suggest that the answer turns on the constitutional value attributed to the circulation of expert knowledge. It is the job of attorneys to advise clients about how best to navigate the legal options available to them. It is the expectation of clients that they will receive this advice. The plain language of BAPCPA interrupts these mutual expectations about the circulation of legal knowledge. As interpreted in lower federal courts, BAPCPA prohibits attorneys from communicating genuine legal knowledge about possible legal action. Precisely the vulnerability and dependence of clients makes this prohibition all the more damaging. The Supreme Court sidestepped this prohibition by narrowly interpreting BAPCPA to apply only to attorney communications advising actions otherwise prohibited by law.

A growing number of legal commentators have offered an explanation for the First Amendment coverage BAPCPA inspired in lower courts. These commentators embrace what is now called an "institutional approach to the First Amendment."[81] The basic idea is that the First Amendment ought to protect the "defined social relationships" that make up existing institutions, such as the profession of law.[82] Applied literally, this approach suggests that the First Amendment coverage should be triggered by any political regulation of extant professional practices. BAPCPA, as interpreted in lower federal courts, sought to subordinate existing attorney-client relationships to political control.

I regard the premise of the institutional approach as implausible. It is often necessary or desirable to exert political control over professional practices, and such control necessitates the regulation of professional communication. A constitutional theory that immediately converts every effort to regulate professional practice into a constitutional question is surely suspect. It is also misleading. We know that professional practices are subject to many regulations, like ordinary malpractice law, that do not trigger First Amendment coverage. The institutional approach thus obscures the central puzzle that we must explain, which is why some political efforts to regulate professional practices, like BAPCPA, seem to trigger First Amendment coverage, while other efforts, like malpractice law, do not.

The approach I have outlined in this book suggests a solution to this puzzle. Some regulations of professional practices implicate First Amendment values, whereas others do not. This is inconsistent with the major premise of the institutional approach, which attributes constitutional value to professional practices as such. I suggest that a more nuanced inquiry is required, one which will evaluate whether particular government regulations threaten particular constitutional values.[83]

What First Amendment values might be implicated in the particular kinds of attorney-client communications regulated by BAPCPA? These values cannot inhere in the autonomy of attorneys, because attorney speech is pervasively regulated without triggering First Amendment coverage. An attorney who fails to advise her client about a legal and potentially useful enlargement of debt in contemplation of bankruptcy might be liable in malpractice, and yet she cannot invoke the First Amendment to defend against such a suit. The constitutional values threatened by BAPCPA do not lie in attorney speech "as such," nor in the marketplace of ideas. Attorneys are regularly and uncontroversially held strictly responsible for the truth and accuracy of their opinions.[84]

I can see no alternative but to conclude that lower federal courts understood BAPCPA to trigger First Amendment coverage because they believed that its purpose and effect was to block the communication of knowledge that might ultimately inform public opinion and thereby enhance the competency of democratic decision-making. As with commercial speech, it does not matter that this knowledge is communicated outside public discourse.

This analysis has the virtue of explaining why malpractice litigation does not trigger First Amendment coverage. Malpractice litigation regulates professional speech in order to maintain pertinent professional criteria of knowledge. The question in a malpractice suit is whether a professional has met professional standards in the communication of knowledge. Malpractice litigation is thus a vehicle for law to incorporate and enforce pertinent disciplinary standards.[85] Just as the regulation of "misleading" commercial speech is exempt from First Amendment review,[86] so the regulation of professional malpractice is beyond First Amendment coverage.[87]

In contrast to malpractice litigation, legislation like BAPCPA seeks to politically override relevant professional standards of knowledge. Legislation like BAPCPA can compromise the constitutional value of democratic competence when it prohibits professional experts from communicating knowledge that is professionally regarded as true. Legislation that requires professional experts to communicate knowledge that is professionally regarded as false should for this same reason also trigger First Amendment coverage, as has happened in Nebraska. In such circumstances First Amendment coverage is triggered because the value of democratic competence is at risk.

III.

If First Amendment coverage is triggered by statutes that prevent professionals from communicating relevant disciplinary knowledge to clients, or that force professionals to communicate untruths to clients, the scope of First Amendment coverage must depend upon judicial assessment of the relevant state of expert knowledge. This has subtle but highly significant constitutional implications.

Consider a dentist who wishes to advise her patients to remove their dental amalgams and who is prohibited from doing so by local regulation.[88] Imagine that the dentist charges that the regulation violates the First Amendment. The question of whether the regulation blocks the transmission of knowledge and hence triggers First Amendment coverage depends upon whether dental amalgams actually endanger the health of patients. How can a court answer this question? It must necessarily apply the disciplinary knowledge of medical experts. It follows that First Amendment coverage depends upon the application of the very disciplinary practices that government regulation seeks to control. A court will have no option but to apply the authoritative methods and truths of medical science in order to determine whether prohibiting the dentist's advice triggers First Amendment review.

It follows that the value of democratic competence can be judicially protected only if courts incorporate and apply the disciplinary methods by which expert knowledge is defined. This is the kernel of truth at the core of the new institutional approach to the First Amendment. Constitutional protections for the circulation of expert knowledge, in contrast to commercial information, require courts to apply the disciplinary methods by which disciplinary knowledge is itself ascertained.

These disciplinary methods are neither democratic nor egalitarian. They are not to be determined by popular vote.

Although courts cannot adopt these disciplinary methods to regulate public discourse, they can and must use them to assess the constitutionality of legislative efforts to regulate the circulation of expert knowledge outside of public discourse. In the context of BAPCPA, for example, lower courts applied First Amendment scrutiny because the statute prevented lawyers from communicating to clients legal knowledge of their right to incur debt in contemplation of bankruptcy; courts agreed that this claim of legal knowledge was true by virtue of their own application of the disciplinary practices that establish legal truth.

The implications of this analysis are startling. Protecting the value of democratic competence will, in the context of expert knowledge, require courts to attribute constitutional status to the disciplinary practices by which expert knowledge is itself created. Courts must adopt and employ such practices whenever they seek to safeguard the circulation of disciplinary knowledge. It follows that judicial efforts to safeguard the value of democratic competence ultimately depend upon a constitutional sociology of knowledge.

Consider what would happen if a state were to pass legislation prohibiting astrologers from offering fee-for-service advice to clients.[89] The state would defend its legislation on the ground that such advice constitutes consumer fraud.[90] Ordinary consumer fraud is prohibited without triggering First Amendment coverage[91] because anti-fraud legislation is understood to suppress falsehood rather than truth. Outside of public discourse, First Amendment scrutiny is not triggered by the censorship of deceptions, only by the suppression of actual knowledge or information.[92]

If we ask how a court might determine whether astrological advice constitutes deception or knowledge, we must identify the body of expertise which a court would use in order to
answer this question. It is all but certain that a court would not
decide whether astrological advice communicates knowledge
by consulting the disciplinary standards of astrology. A court
would instead consult what it regards as reliable forms of disciplinary expertise,[93] in much the same way that lower courts
considering the constitutionality of BAPCPA consulted the
disciplinary standards of the legal profession to determine
whether the statute interrupted the communication of legal
knowledge.

In our society the professional practices of lawyers produce the kind of knowledge that advances the value of democratic competence, but the professional practices of astrologers
do not. It is reasonable to plan to rely on legal advice, but it
is foolish to plan to rely on astrological opinion. That is why
the scope of First Amendment coverage depends upon the application of the disciplinary practices of lawyers, but not upon
the disciplinary practices of astrologers. The value of democratic competence is potentially at risk only if the state com-
promises the transmission of actual knowledge. Determining
which disciplinary practices produce knowledge, and which
do not, inevitably entangles constitutional adjudication in the
sociological construction of knowledge.

The case of astrology is relatively simple, but consider a
more complex example. Suppose a state were to prohibit persons from offering fee-for-service advice about a particular
homeopathic medical remedy. The disciplinary status of homeopathic medicine is highly controverted.[94] How will a court

decide whether the prohibition of advice about the remedy triggers First Amendment coverage? A court may believe that the discipline of homeopathic medicine produces valuable knowledge, in which case it will decide the question of First Amendment coverage by reference to experts in homeopathic medicine. Such a court will ask whether experts in homeopathic medicine would or would not approve the homeopathic remedy at issue. If homeopathic specialists agree that the remedy is fraudulent, First Amendment coverage will not be triggered. If they believe that the remedy is effective, then the suppression will trigger First Amendment coverage in exactly the same way as First Amendment coverage was triggered by BAPCPA.

A court may also believe, however, that homeopathic medicine is like astrology, because it is a discipline that does not itself produce constitutionally valuable knowledge. Such a court will determine whether the prohibition of advice about the homeopathic remedy suppresses the circulation of knowledge by applying the expertise of an "established" scientific discipline. If "established" experts agree that the remedy is effective, First Amendment coverage may be triggered, whereas if "established" experts agree that the remedy is fraudulent, no First Amendment question will be presented.[95]

The point is that although courts may retain the option of accepting or rejecting the specific disciplinary practices of homeopathic medicine, they will not retain the option of avoiding *all* disciplinary practices. Ultimately a court must determine whether First Amendment coverage is triggered by deciding whether prohibiting advice about the remedy does or does not suppress the circulation of knowledge. And it must make this determination by applying the methods of one dis-

cipline or another. Whatever discipline a court applies will
acquire constitutional status, because it will determine the forms
of knowledge implicating the constitutional value of democratic competence.

Insofar as the value of democratic competence safeguards
the circulation of expert knowledge, it must necessarily also
incorporate the disciplinary methods by which expert knowledge is created and certified. A constitutional sociology of
knowledge is thus inevitable. This sociology will pose deep
and intractable questions. Consider, for example, what a court
might do if the federal government were to enact legislation
requiring accountants to report financial returns to their clients using only predetermined federal formulae for the calculation of profit.[96] Such legislation seeks to control the professional advice of accountants. If the legislation were challenged
under the First Amendment, coverage would be triggered if
the mandated federal formulae either prevented accountants
from distributing knowledge or required accountants to distribute falsehoods. How might a court determine whether federal formulae had these consequences?

If a court regards the practices of accountants as consti-
tutive of financial knowledge,[97] it will likely take legislative efforts to override the disciplinary practices of professional accountants as triggering serious First Amendment questions,
just as courts considering the constitutionality of BAPCPA
took the attempt to override the legal knowledge of lawyers to
raise serious First Amendment questions. But a different issue
would be presented if a court instead regards the expertise of
accountants to be merely that of representing financial knowledge,[98] the truth of which is to be determined by the practices

of "established" disciplines like economics. Such a court would have to determine the boundaries of First Amendment coverage by applying the knowledge practices of economists. These knowledge practices would accordingly acquire independent constitutional status.

IV.

The argument of this chapter is that there are indeed strong suggestions in First Amendment doctrine that courts are willing to protect the value of democratic competence. We can detect the influence of democratic competence whenever courts protect the circulation of information outside of public discourse in the context of commercial speech, or whenever courts protect the circulation of expert knowledge outside of public discourse in contexts like BAPCPA. When courts protect the circulation of expert knowledge, they also extend constitutional recognition to the disciplinary practices and methods that create such knowledge. In effect this immunizes such practices and methods from unrestricted political manipulation.

The doctrinal structure I have identified safeguards the independence of key liberal institutions that produce expert knowledge. This structure does not compromise democratic legitimation by subordinating public discourse to approved disciplinary practices and truths. It preserves the autonomy of public discourse, even as it sustains democratic competence by maintaining separation between the "sphere of knowledge" and the "sphere of power." It prevents the state from obliterating independent sources of expert knowledge. By ascribing constitutional status to the independent disciplinary practices that define expert knowledge, it empowers democratic citizens to demand accountability from their government. Whether any particular disciplinary practice will acquire constitutional status of this kind depends upon the constitutional sociology of knowledge.

3

Academic Freedom and the Production of Disciplinary Knowledge

The value of democratic competence is undermined whenever the state acts to interrupt the communication of disciplinary knowledge that might inform the creation of public opinion. Lower federal courts extended First Amendment coverage to BAPCPA because they considered the statute to have this purpose and effect. The question I address in this chapter is whether existing First Amendment doctrine seeks to safeguard the value of democratic competence by extending First Amendment coverage also to state actions that inhibit the *creation* of expert knowledge.

There is an obvious candidate for such doctrine. First Amendment jurisprudence has protected academic freedom for more than fifty years. Academic freedom safeguards the creation of disciplinary knowledge within universities. The Supreme Court has proclaimed that academic freedom is a "special concern of the First Amendment, which does not tolerate laws that cast a pall of orthodoxy over the classroom."[1]

At present, however, the doctrine of academic freedom stands in a state of shocking disarray and incoherence. One eminent commentator has remarked that "there has been no adequate analysis of what academic freedom the Constitution protects or of why it protects it. Lacking definition or guiding principle, the doctrine floats in the law, picking up decisions as a hull does barnacles."[2]

The problem is in part that the Court has failed to understand the connection between academic freedom and the value of democratic competence. It has instead sought to protect academic freedom in order to safeguard the marketplace of ideas. It has announced that "[t]he classroom is peculiarly the 'marketplace of ideas.' The Nation's future depends upon leaders trained through wide exposure to that robust exchange of ideas which discovers truth 'out of a multitude of tongues, (rather) than through any kind of authoritative selection.'"[3]

If the purpose of constitutional protections for academic freedom is to serve the value of democratic competence, the ideal of the marketplace of ideas can only produce confusion. Universities are essential institutions for the creation of disciplinary knowledge, and such knowledge is produced by discriminating between good and bad ideas. It follows that academic freedom cannot usefully be conceptualized as protecting a marketplace of ideas. In this chapter I shall argue that constitutional safeguards for academic freedom are best justified in terms of the value of democratic competence and that this perspective can helpfully illuminate many of the conundrums that presently afflict judicial efforts to construct the First Amendment doctrine of academic freedom.

I.

Today we are likely to find unexceptionable, perhaps even banal, Karl Jaspers's claim that "the university is the corporate realization of man's basic determination to know. Its most immediate aim is to discover what there is to be known and what becomes of us through knowledge."[4] Almost every modern university includes in its mission statement the purpose of striving "to create knowledge."[5] The modern university is defined in terms of "the preservation, advancement, and dissemination of knowledge."[6] Universities are institutions that paradigmatically develop and apply the disciplinary practices that define modern forms of expert knowledge.

This concept of the university did not always exist in the United States. During the major part of the nineteenth century, the objective of most American colleges was to instruct young men in received truths, both spiritual and material. It is only when American scholars became infected with the German ideal of *Wissenschaft,* with the idea of systematizing and expanding knowledge, that American universities began to transform their mission. It is a moment of great historical significance when Daniel Coit Gilman could in 1885 address the assembled officers, students, and friends of the John Hopkins University to assert, with confidence and at length, that the "functions" of the university "may be stated as the acquisition, conservation, refinement and distribution of knowledge. . . . It is the business of a university to advance knowledge."[7]

The concept of academic freedom emerged in the United States in response to this transformation of the purpose of higher education.[8] Writing during this moment of transition,

John Dewey could with characteristic lucidity observe the emerging relationship between the new concept of the university and the new idea of academic freedom:

> In discussing the questions summed up in the phrase academic freedom, it is necessary to make a distinction between the university proper and those teaching bodies, called by whatever name, whose primary business is to inculcate a fixed set of ideas and facts. The former aims to discover and communicate truth and to make its recipients better judges of truth and more effective in applying it to the affairs of life. The latter have as their aim the perpetuation of a certain way of looking at things current among a given body of persons. Their purpose is to disciple rather than to discipline. . . . The problem of freedom of inquiry and instruction clearly assumes different forms in these two types of institutions.[9]

The basic idea of academic freedom is simple and unanswerable: knowledge cannot be advanced unless existing claims to knowledge can with freedom be criticized and analyzed.[10] Arthur Lovejoy elegantly summarized the point in 1930, noting that the university's

> function of seeking new truths will sometimes mean . . . the undermining of widely or generally accepted beliefs. It is rendered impossible if the work of the investigator is shackled by the requirement that his

conclusions shall never seriously deviate either from generally accepted beliefs or from those accepted by the persons, private or official, through whom society provides the means for the maintenance of universities. . . . Academic freedom is, then, a prerequisite condition to the proper prosecution, in an organized and adequately endowed manner, of scientific inquiry. . . .[11]

The first and arguably greatest articulation of the logic and structure of academic freedom in America was the *1915 Declaration of Principles on Academic Freedom and Academic Tenure,* published by the newly formed American Association of University Professors (AAUP).[12] The concept of academic freedom advanced in the *Declaration* was later incorporated in the canonical *1940 Statement of Principles on Academic Freedom and Tenure,*[13] which has been endorsed by over 180 educational organizations and which has become "the general norm of academic practice in the United States."[14]

The *1915 Declaration* defined academic freedom as consisting of three components: "Academic freedom . . . comprises three elements: freedom of inquiry and research; freedom of teaching within the university or college; and freedom of extramural utterance and action."[15] Twenty-five years later these same three components of academic freedom were reaffirmed in the *1940 Statement.*[16] In this chapter I shall analyze the constitutional dimensions of the first of these three components, which the *1940 Statement* characterizes as freedom of research and publication.[17] Insofar as the constitutional value of democratic competence concerns the creation and dissemination of disciplinary knowledge, it concerns this first component of academic freedom.

It is apparent that the *1915 Declaration* does not analogize academic freedom of research and publication to the marketplace of ideas. The *Declaration* does indeed argue that because a purpose of higher education is "to promote inquiry and advance the sum of human knowledge,"[18] universities must award faculty with "complete and unlimited freedom to pursue inquiry and publish its results. Such freedom is the breath in the nostrils of all scientific activity."[19] But although the *Declaration* asserts that "the university teacher's independence of thought and utterance"[20] is required by the basic purpose of a university, it also takes pains to distinguish this independence of thought from a marketplace of ideas in which all ideas must be tolerated.

The *Declaration* explicitly repudiates the position "that academic freedom implies that individual teachers should be exempt from all restraints as to the matter or manner of their utterances, either within or without the university."[21] Academic freedom implies that the "liberty of the scholar within the university to set forth his conclusions, be they what they may, is conditioned by their being conclusions gained by a scholar's method and held in a scholar's spirit; that is to say, they must be the fruits of competent and patient and sincere inquiry."[22] The *Declaration* conceives academic freedom as the freedom to pursue the "scholar's profession"[23] according to the standards of that profession.[24] It is only in this way that scholars can fulfill the university's mission of creating new knowledge.

In contrast to the marketplace of ideas, therefore, academic freedom protects scholarly speech only when it complies with "professional norms."[25] It is for this reason that universities are free to evaluate scholarly speech based upon its content—to reward or to regulate scholarly speech based upon its professional quality.[26] Universities make these judgments whenever they hire professors, promote them, tenure them, or award them grants. Although the First Amendment would prohibit government from regulating the *New York Times* if the newspaper were inclined to editorialize that the moon is made of green cheese, no astronomy department could survive if it were prevented from denying tenure to a young scholar who was similarly convinced. Academic freedom thus depends upon a double recognition: that knowledge cannot be advanced "in the absence of free inquiry," and that "the right question to ask about a teacher is whether he is competent."[27]

Competence is defined by reference to scholarly or disciplinary standards. These standards cannot be determined by reference to public opinion.[28] "The definition of competence does not shift with every wind of prejudice, religious, political, racial, or economic."[29] Academic freedom has always been conceived as a barrier to "the pressure in a democracy of a concentrated multitudinous public opinion. The great majority of the people in a given community may hold passionately to some dogma in religion, some economic doctrine, or some political or social opinion or practice, and may resent strongly the expression by a public teacher of religious, economic, political, or social views unlike those held by the majority."[30] Academic freedom insulates scholars from the political pressure of public opinion so that they can pursue the disciplinary practices by which expert knowledge is created and certified.[31] Academic freedom, as the *Declaration* precisely notes, upholds "not the absolute freedom of utterance of the individual scholar, but the absolute freedom of thought, of inquiry, of discussion and of teaching, of the academic profession."[32]

This concept of academic freedom initially developed as a professional norm for the governance of institutions of higher education. It was not recognized in constitutional law during the first half of the twentieth century. In 1937, for example, a legal commentator could note that "academic freedom is not . . . a constitutional privilege, or even a legal term defined by a history of judicial usage and separately listed in the digests and *Words and Phrases.*"[33] Academic freedom did not emerge as a constitutional concept until the 1950s and McCarthyite efforts to remove subversives from the nation's universities.[34] It was not until 1967 that we learned that academic freedom is a "special concern of the First Amendment."[35] The question I shall explore in this chapter is exactly why academic freedom should be of concern to the First Amendment and how that concern ought doctrinally to be expressed.[36]

II.

To speak of academic freedom as a First Amendment right is to presuppose that academic freedom serves a specifically constitutional value. Universities and university faculty are the unique and primary sites in modern American society for the creation and diffusion of disciplinary knowledge in the service of the public good. Creating and diffusing disciplinary knowledge serves the First Amendment value of democratic competence. It is exactly this value that the Court invoked when it initially began to speak of academic freedom as a constitutional principle.

The first major Supreme Court decision to invoke the concept of academic freedom was *Sweezy v. New Hampshire.*[37] The case concerned a New Hampshire "loyalty program" designed "to eliminate 'subversive persons' among government personnel."[38] The state attorney general sought to interrogate Paul Sweezy, a well-known Marxist economist who had been a visiting lecturer at the University of New Hampshire. Sweezy answered all the attorney general's questions with the exception of inquiries about two subjects: "his lectures at the University of New Hampshire, and his knowledge of the Progressive Party and its adherents."[39] Sweezy's support of Henry Wallace's Progressive Party involved his participation in public discourse, and no theory of academic freedom was necessary in order to understand that the attorney general's investigation had impinged "upon such highly sensitive areas as . . . freedom of political association."[40]

But Sweezy's classroom lectures on "the theory of dialectical materialism" or the inevitability of "Socialism" were quite another matter.[41] These lectures formed no part of public discourse, because Sweezy's relationship to the students in his classroom constituted a professional relationship, analogous to the relationship between a lawyer and her clients. Sweezy could properly have been held accountable for the professional competence of his lectures.[42] If the attorney general's attempted interrogation of Sweezy's lectures triggered First Amendment coverage, it was not because Sweezy had the First

Amendment right to influence public opinion as he saw fit. The classroom is not a location in which the value of democratic legitimation is at stake.

In his plurality opinion, therefore, Chief Justice Warren was forced to develop a distinct justification for extending First Amendment coverage to Sweezy's lectures:

> The essentiality of freedom in the community of American universities is almost self-evident. No one should underestimate the vital role in a democracy that is played by those who guide and train our youth. To impose any strait jacket upon the intellectual leaders in our colleges and universities would imperil the future of our Nation. No field of education is so thoroughly comprehended by man that new discoveries cannot yet be made. Particularly is that true in the social sciences, where few, if any, principles are accepted as absolutes. Scholarship cannot flourish in an atmosphere of suspicion and distrust. Teachers and students must always remain free to inquire, to study and to evaluate, to gain new maturity and understanding; otherwise our civilization will stagnate and die.[43]

The passage is blurry, invoking both freedom of teaching and freedom of research. It is upon the latter that I wish to focus. In this regard Warren emphasizes the need for American "democracy" to avoid the stagnation that would occur were it to fail to make "new discoveries." It conceives "scholarship" as a medium for these discoveries, especially "in the social sciences," and it concludes that democratic competence in this regard must be protected by awarding teachers the freedom "to inquire, to study and to evaluate, to gain new maturity and understanding."

In his influential concurring opinion, Justice Frankfurter was even more explicit:

> Progress in the natural sciences is not remotely confined to findings made in the laboratory. Insights into the mysteries of nature are born of hypothesis and speculation. The more so is this true in the pursuit of understanding in the groping endeavors of what are called the social sciences, the concern of which is man and society. The problems that are the respective preoccupations of anthropology, economics, law, psychology, sociology and related areas of scholarship are merely departmentalized dealing, by way of manageable division of analysis, with interpenetrating aspects of holistic perplexities. For society's good—if understanding be an essential need of society—inquiries into these problems, speculations about them, stimulation in others of reflection upon them, must be left as unfettered as possible. Political power must abstain from intrusion into this activity of freedom, pursued in the interest of wise government and the people's well-being, except for reasons that are exigent and obviously compelling.[44]

Frankfurter quoted extensively from the statement of a conference of senior South African scholars in defense of open universities:

"A university is characterized by the spirit of free inquiry, its ideal being the ideal of Socrates—'to follow the argument where it leads.' This implies the right to examine, question, modify or reject traditional ideas and beliefs. Dogma and hypothesis are incompatible, and the concept of an immutable doctrine is repugnant to the spirit of a university. . . .

"Freedom to reason and freedom for disputation on the basis of observation and experiment are the necessary conditions for the advancement of scientific knowledge. A sense of freedom is also necessary for creative work in the arts which, equally with scientific research, is the concern of the university.

". . . It is the business of a university to provide that atmosphere which is most conducive to speculation, experiment and creation. It is an atmosphere in which there prevail 'the four essential freedoms' of a university—to determine for itself on academic grounds who may teach, what may be taught, how it shall be taught, and who may be admitted to study.'"[45]

These passages justify a First Amendment doctrine of academic freedom on the ground that universities, and the scholars who populate them, produce "understanding," and that understanding is "an essential need of society." Disciplinary knowledge can be acquired only through "hypothesis and speculation." The value of democratic competence thus lies at the root of the constitutionalization of academic freedom of research and inquiry. As we saw in Chapter Two, expert knowledge is a constitutional value in a democracy that depends upon public opinion.

The value of democratic competence plays out differently in the context of academic freedom than in the framework of professional speech. There are at least two salient distinctions. First, doctors and lawyers do not possess academic freedom; instead the law of malpractice rigorously requires them to transmit existing pertinent expert knowledge to patients and clients. Although we may demand competence from professional scholars, academic freedom is deliberately designed to provide ample room for experimentation and speculation that may "seriously deviate either from generally accepted beliefs or from those accepted by the persons, private or official, through whom society provides the means for the maintenance of universities."[46]

This difference is explained by the fact that we require doctors and lawyers to maintain existing standards of knowledge, whereas we expect scholars to create *new* knowledge. Universities cannot expand knowledge if faculty merely reproduce already existing knowledge. There is thus a tension built into the core of academic freedom between, on the one hand, expanding the frontiers of existing knowledge, and, on the other hand, competently exemplifying existing disciplinary standards. This tension, which has no analogue in the context of professional speech, is persistent and without resolution.[47] The tension is practically mediated by the distinction between untenured faculty, who are closely scrutinized for competence, and tenured faculty, who are awarded a generous presumption of competence to facilitate the academic freedom necessary for creating new knowledge.

Second, academic freedom refers not only to the freedom of faculty, but also to the specific institution of the university. There is no real analogy to this concrete institutional focus in the context of professional speech. In his *Sweezy* concurrence, for example, Frankfurter speaks of "'the four essential freedoms' of a university—to determine for itself on academic grounds who may teach, what may be taught, how it shall be taught, and who may be admitted to study." Frankfurter's remarks have greatly influenced subsequent cases like *Regents of the University of California v. Bakke*[48] and *Grutter v. Bollinger*,[49] which have tended to identify academic freedom with the institutional autonomy of universities.

Although new disciplinary knowledge can be generated at innumerable social sites, the constitutional emphasis on universities expresses the idea that academic freedom protects not research as such, but rather the disinterested scholarship established by institutions of higher education. Private corporations may invest in the creation of new expert knowledge, but they do not do so for the public good, as do universities. This point was emphasized more than a decade before *Sweezy* in Vannevar Bush's influential 1945 report to President Truman about the need to provide government support for basic scientific research.[50] Stressing that "without scientific progress no amount of achievement in other directions can insure our health, prosperity, and security as a nation in the modern world,"[51] Bush flatly concluded that

> Publicly and privately supported colleges and universities and the endowed research institutes must furnish both the new scientific knowledge and the trained

research workers. These institutions are uniquely qualified by tradition and by their special characteristics to carry on basic research. They are charged with the responsibility of conserving the knowledge accumulated by the past, imparting that knowledge to students, and contributing new knowledge of all kinds. It is chiefly in these institutions that scientists may work in an atmosphere which is relatively free from the adverse pressure of convention, prejudice, or commercial necessity. At their best they provide the scientific worker with a strong sense of solidarity and security, as well as a substantial degree of personal intellectual freedom. All of these factors are of great importance in the development of new knowledge, since much of new knowledge is certain to arouse opposition because of its tendency to challenge current beliefs or practices.

Industry is generally inhibited by preconceived goals, by its own clearly defined standards, and by the constant pressure of commercial necessity. Satisfactory progress in basic science seldom occurs under conditions prevailing in the normal industrial laboratory. There are some notable exceptions, it is true, but even in such cases it is rarely possible to match the university in respect to the freedom which is so important to scientific discovery.[52]

In the contemporary United States, universities are unique institutions. Not only do universities foster the *disinterested* pursuit of disciplinary knowledge, but they are also the institutions distinctively authorized to define, nourish, and reproduce disciplines themselves. Disciplines may be practiced in private corporate settings, but they are articulated, replenished, and sustained in universities.[53] Through their virtual monopoly of graduate training, universities certify experts, as well as their expertise. "Disciplines" that flourish outside universities, like astrology, are unlikely to be accepted as reliable.

Recognizing the interdependence of reliable disciplinary knowledge and institutions of higher education, the Court in *Sweezy* invested universities with distinct constitutional value. This institutional focus was so intense that the Court regarded it as irrelevant that Paul Sweezy himself, although an economist of note and reputation, was not a tenured member of any university faculty, but merely a guest lecturer in a classroom. What mattered was that Sweezy was participating in the disciplinary training appropriate to a university setting.

The sharp focus on the institutional significance of universities can at times seem to contradict the conclusion that individual professors might possess academic freedom. Consider what might have happened if Sweezy had been on the faculty of the University of New Hampshire and had been disciplined by the university administration in order to assuage political pressure coming from university alums. If Sweezy were to sue for a violation of academic freedom, and if the University of New Hampshire were to defend on the ground of its own institutional autonomy—the university's own academic freedom to supervise its faculty—a latent tension between individual and institutional academic freedom would seem to become manifest.

Courts[54] and commentators[55] have noticed this potential

conflict between individual and institutional concepts of academic freedom, and they have spilled a great deal of ink over the question of which form of academic freedom ought to be adopted by courts. But the tension between individual and institutional academic freedom can be reconciled if we appreciate that the function of First Amendment doctrine is to protect First Amendment values, and that the First Amendment value at stake in academic freedom of research and publication is democratic competence.[56] This value encompasses *both* the ongoing health of universities as institutions that promote the growth of disciplinary knowledge *and* the capacity of individual scholars to promote and disseminate the results of disciplinary inquiry.

Universities foster the growth of new expert knowledge by facilitating scholarship that reproduces, applies, and improves disciplinary practices. That is why American university administrators typically and properly defer heavily to the peer judgments of faculty when making decisions about academic competence. If administrators were instead to defer to "the prevailing opinions and sentiments of the community in which they dwell," and thus to override professional standards in the name of "this multitudinous tyrannical opinion,"[57] universities as institutions would cease to serve the constitutional value of democratic competence. They would become, in the words of the *1915 Declaration*, "essentially proprietary institutions" which do not

> accept the principles of freedom of inquiry, of opinion, and of teaching; . . . [T]heir purpose [would not be] to advance knowledge by the unrestricted research

and unfettered discussion of impartial investigators, but rather to subsidize the promotion of opinions held by the persons, usually not of the scholar's calling, who provide the funds for their maintenance.[58]

It is "manifestly important," the *Declaration* asserts, that such faux universities "not be permitted to sail under false colors."[59]

From a constitutional point of view, therefore, academic freedom has nothing to do with the autonomy of institutions that happen to include the name "university" in their titles. It applies instead only to institutions that facilitate the application and improvement of professional scholarly standards to advance knowledge for the public good.[60] Academic freedom does not entail deference to university administrators "who have expertise in education."[61] It instead entails deference to the professional scholarly standards through which knowledge is created.

Consider what would happen if Paul Sweezy had been a tenured professor at the University of New Hampshire and if his lectures had been suppressed by his colleagues in the economics department because they regarded his economic views as professionally inadequate. Because peer evaluation is always a necessary precondition for academic freedom, Sweezy could have sued for redress only on the ground that the sanction imposed by his peers was incompetent when measured by the professional standards of the discipline of economics. Sweezy would in effect have had to ask a court to determine that his peers had failed properly to apply the prevailing standards of the economics community. The ultimate object of a court's inquiry would have to be the proper application of professional scholarly standards. These standards determine the boundaries of academic freedom. These boundaries are blurry because the whole purpose of academic freedom is to encourage experimentation, hypothesis, and speculation. The distinction between competent and incompetent economics scholarship is a great deal more murky than the distinction between competent and incompetent medicine or legal advice. It is for this reason plausible for courts to have concluded that

> [w]hen judges are asked to review the substance of a genuinely academic decision . . . they should show great respect for the faculty's professional judgment. Plainly, they may not override it unless it is such a substantial departure from accepted academic norms as to demonstrate that the person or committee responsible did not actually exercise professional judgment.[62]

The justification for deference is that courts are not well equipped to second-guess the exercise of the professional scholarly standards that advance the constitutional value of democratic competence in the context of university scholarship. Courts are properly concerned that "judges should not be ersatz deans and educators."[63] Nothing in this concept of academic freedom, however, justifies deference when universities make executive decisions that do not purport to reflect professional standards.[64] Nothing in the concept of academic freedom requires deference to university administrators who possess neither the capacity nor the pretense of exercising professional judgment.

This suggests that the supposed tension between the institutional and individual accounts of academic freedom is based upon a misunderstanding. The constitutional value of academic freedom depends upon the exercise of professional standards, which inhere neither in institutions as such, nor in individual professors as such. The right question for courts to ask about academic freedom is how to fashion doctrine that best protects the "freedom of thought, of inquiry . . . of the academic profession."[65] This can be a complicated question, because administrative decision-makers often purport to rely on professional standards. It is important, however, not to confuse the question of when deference is appropriate with the question of whether academic freedom inheres in institutions or in individuals.[66]

III.

Without doubt the most controversial recent decision involving academic freedom has been *Urofsky v. Gilmore,*[67] decided en banc by the Fourth Circuit in 2000. The case concerns a challenge to a Virginia statute providing that state employees, including university professors, cannot "access, download, print or store information infrastructure files or servers having sexually explicit content," unless such access is approved in writing by an "agency head."[68] *Gilmore* realized that the statute, because it restricts the research of faculty, is inconsistent with academic freedom conceived as "a professional norm,"[69] but it concluded that "[t]he Supreme Court, to the extent it has constitutionalized a right of academic freedom at all, appears to have recognized only an institutional right of self-governance in academic affairs" rather than "a First Amendment right of academic freedom that belongs to the professor as an individual."[70] *Gilmore* did not seem to realize that if the Supreme Court had indeed articulated a constitutional right of academic freedom that attached to universities, it was to serve the constitutional value of democratic competence, which is straightforwardly implicated by the need of individual professors to pursue professional research free from government interference.[71]

Gilmore was explicit that "because the Act does not infringe the constitutional rights of public employees in general, it also does not violate the rights of professors."[72] *Gilmore* analyzed the constitutional rights of public employees in terms of Supreme Court precedents like *Pickering v. Board of Education,*[73] *Connick v. Myers,*[74] and *Waters v. Churchill.*[75] These decisions hold that First Amendment coverage does not extend to the regulation of state employee speech unless such speech involves "a matter of public concern."[76] *Gilmore* is unusual because it frankly acknowledges that the "public concern" test of the *Pickering-Connick-Churchill* line of cases refers to general First Amendment rights that have nothing especially to do with academic freedom. But this point has not generally been recognized by courts, which have instead regularly used the "public concern" test to assess whether state regulations infringe academic freedom.[77] This use of the test represents a deep misunderstanding of the nature of academic freedom of research and publication.[78]

The *Pickering-Connick-Churchill* line of cases rests on the premise that in a democracy the implementation of government decisions frequently requires the creation of organizations. If a democratic state wishes to create a social security system, it must establish a social security administration; if it wishes to provide a welfare system, it must establish a social service bureaucracy. Such organizations are purposive; they exist to achieve the ends for which they are created. Within such organizations, therefore, the state must manage its employees, including their speech, in ways designed to fulfill organizational objectives. The point is quite general. Not only must the speech of bureaucrats be regulated so as to attain bureaucratic ends, but the speech of soldiers must be regulated so as to secure the national defense, and the speech of lawyers within a courtroom must be regulated so as to secure justice.[79] "The state has interests as an employer in regulating the speech of its employees that differ significantly from those it possesses in connection with the regulation of the speech of the citizenry in general."[80]

When an employee speaks about a matter of "public concern," however, she participates in public discourse "as a citizen."[81] In such instances, the state must "balance between the interests of the [employee], as a citizen, in commenting upon matters of public concern and the interest of the State, as an employer, in promoting the efficiency of the public services it performs through its employees."[82] The instrumental logic of an organization must somehow be reconciled with the egalitarian structure of public discourse. The *Pickering-Connick-Churchill* line of cases is about how this reconciliation should be effected.

The structure of faculty speech within public universities is subject to a similar analysis. The speech of faculty within state universities can be regulated as is necessary to achieve the purposes of higher education.[83] But university faculty may also wish to participate in public discourse as citizens. It is precisely this tension that the Court in *Sweezy* addresses when it condemns the New Hampshire attorney general for questioning Paul Sweezy about his involvement in the Progressive Party. The Court concludes that Paul Sweezy's participation in the Progressive Party had nothing to do with his employment as a professor, and that his political association could therefore not justify penalizing him in his capacity as a state employee.

The question of academic freedom arises in *Sweezy* only in the context of Sweezy's classroom lectures; it has nothing to do with his participation in the Progressive Party. *Sweezy* conceptualizes the inquiry into Sweezy's party politics as a violation of the "political freedom of the individual."[84] The precise question of Sweezy's academic freedom, by contrast, arises because the New Hampshire attorney general sought to chill Sweezy's classroom lectures. In these lectures Sweezy did not play the role of a citizen; he was not participating in public discourse.[85] He was an expert communicating knowledge to his students and thereby to the public. It was his function as a university employee to communicate this knowledge. The state attorney general's interrogation threatened to suppress *both* Sweezy's communication of expert knowledge to the public *and* Sweezy's ability to function effectively in a state organization.

Academic freedom of research and publication concerns the special function of university faculty to expand the frontiers of disciplinary knowledge. Academic freedom is covered by the First Amendment not because of the value of democratic legitimation, but because of the value of democratic competence. Because the criterion of "public concern" is about reconciling the value of democratic legitimation with the value of organizational effectiveness, it should have nothing to do with triggering First Amendment coverage in matters of academic freedom. The "public concern" test is entirely misplaced in an academic freedom inquiry. First Amendment coverage should be triggered whenever the freedom of the scholarly profession to engage in research and publication is potentially compromised. That freedom is necessary both to the effective functioning of state universities and to the realization of the constitutional value of democratic competence.

If the "public concern" test of the *Pickering-Connick-Churchill* line of cases is relevant to anything, it is to the third component of professional academic freedom, which is what the *1915 Declaration* called "freedom of extramural utterance and action."[86] This aspect of professional academic freedom refers to the freedom to "speak or write as citizens"[87] rather than as experts. Freedom of extramural expression might protect an astronomer who wishes to write in public about NAFTA,[88] or a computer scientist who wishes to speak out about the war in Iraq.[89] When faculty engage in such speech, they attempt to influence public opinion so as to make it responsive to their views. They do not speak as experts conveying knowledge, but as citizens participating in public debate.

Experts have for years debated whether freedom of extramural speech should be considered an aspect of professional academic freedom, because freedom of extramural speech is by hypothesis unrelated to the special training and expertise of faculty.[90] From a constitutional point of view, however, freedom of extramural expression raises the same question of democratic legitimation as that which occurs whenever any government employee seeks to participate in public discourse. The "public concern" test of the *Pickering-Connick-Churchill* line of cases is an effort to identify and resolve this question. The question turns on democratic legitimation, and it is therefore fundamentally distinct from the issue of academic freedom of research and publication, which turns on the constitutional value of democratic competence.

The logic of democratic competence unmistakably suggests that regulation of faculty research and publication should trigger First Amendment coverage whether or not faculty speech involves matters of public concern. The general collapse of constitutional academic freedom doctrine into the "public concern" test of the *Pickering-Connick-Churchill* line of cases misses this essential point. It fails to appreciate the independent constitutional value of democratic competence. It fails also to recognize that academic freedom is required to discharge the constitutional mission of state organizations charged with the purpose of expanding knowledge.[91]

IV.

If the "public concern" test is frequently invoked by lower courts attempting to wrestle with thorny questions of constitutional academic freedom, so also is the doctrinal conclusion of another decision of the Supreme Court—*Hazelwood School District v. Kuhlmeier*.[92] In *Hazelwood* the Court held that a secondary school could constitutionally restrict or compel speech as necessary in order to implement its chosen curriculum. In the context of higher education, the holding of *Hazelwood* is typically invoked when a professor claims that a university has interfered with his freedom in the classroom. A good example is *Bishop v. Aronov,*[93] in which a university professor was instructed to refrain from interjecting his religious beliefs during instructional time periods.

Citing *Hazelwood,* the court in *Aronov* held that "[a]s a place of schooling with a teaching mission, we consider the University's authority to reasonably control the content of its curriculum, particularly that content imparted during class time. Tangential to the authority over its curriculum, there lies some authority over the conduct of teachers in and out of the classroom that significantly bears on the curriculum or that gives the appearance of endorsement by the university."[94] The *Aronov* court felt driven to the conclusion that "[t]hough we are mindful of the invaluable role academic freedom plays in our public schools, particularly at the post-secondary level, we do not find support to conclude that academic freedom is an independent First Amendment right."[95]

Most apparently at issue in *Aronov* was the component of academic freedom that the *1915 Declaration* identifies as freedom of teaching.[96] Freedom of teaching is an exceedingly complex and ill-defined topic, for it must be reconciled not only with the capacity of faculty departments and universities to design and implement curricular requirements,[97] but also with the academic freedom of students. If there is an argument for constitutionalizing freedom of teaching, it must be of the kind sketched by Frankfurter in his famous concurrence in *Wieman v. Updegraff:*

That our democracy ultimately rests on public opinion is a platitude of speech but not a commonplace in
action. Public opinion is the ultimate reliance of our
society only if it be disciplined and responsible. It can
be disciplined and responsible only if habits of open-
mindedness and of critical inquiry are acquired in the
formative years of our citizens. The process of education has naturally enough been the basis of hope for
the perdurance of our democracy on the part of all
our great leaders, from Thomas Jefferson onwards.

To regard teachers—in our entire educational system, from the primary grades to the university—as the
priests of our democracy is therefore not to indulge in
hyperbole. It is the special task of teachers to foster
those habits of open-mindedness and critical inquiry
which alone make for responsible citizens, who, in
turn, make possible an enlightened and effective public opinion. Teachers must fulfill their function by pre-
cept and practice, by the very atmosphere which they
generate; they must be exemplars of open-mindedness
and free inquiry. They cannot carry out their noble
task if the conditions for the practice of a responsible
and critical mind are denied to them. They must have
the freedom of responsible inquiry, by thought and
action, into the meaning of social and economic ideas,
into the checkered history of social and economic
dogma. They must be free to sift evanescent doctrine,
qualified by time and circumstance, from that restless,
enduring process of extending the bounds of understanding and wisdom, to assure which the freedoms

of thought, of speech, of inquiry, of worship are guaranteed by the Constitution of the United States against infraction by national or State government.[98]

Frankfurter argues that democracy can succeed only if persons are educated to become competent democratic citizens. The forms of pedagogy necessary for what we may call "democratic education"[99] should thus be invested with constitutional value.[100]

I do not in this chapter address the thorny subject of freedom of teaching.[101] I instead focus on classroom regulations that affect academic freedom of research and publication. This freedom includes the right to disseminate the results of research to the public, including and most especially to students in the classroom. Freedom of research and publication is implicated in the classroom not merely because classrooms are a primary medium for the transmission of scholarly expertise to the public, but also because classrooms are the only medium through which the next generation of disciplinary experts can be produced.

In *Sweezy*, the New Hampshire attorney general sought to inhibit Sweezy's efforts to communicate to his students his scholarly research about the nature of socialism and economic materialism. Academic freedom of research and publication includes, at a minimum, the freedom to communicate the results of research to students when it is pedagogically relevant to do so. Freedom of research does not in this sense seem to have been at issue in *Aronov*, because in that case the professor was teaching a class in "exercise physiology" and the classroom remarks for which he was disciplined concerned how

"God came to earth in the form of Jesus Christ and he has something to tell us about life which is crucial to success and happiness."[102] It is difficult to construe these remarks as a report of scholarly expertise. At most they were an effort to motivate and engage students in the classroom. The remarks may be defended as freedom of teaching, but they cannot reasonably be defended as freedom of research and publication.

In *Sweezy*, by contrast, the State of New Hampshire sought to inhibit a professor from reporting to students pedagogically relevant conclusions of research because the state deemed these conclusions to be irrelevant to issues under consideration in the class. New Hampshire in effect desired to arbitrate economic truth in the classroom and thereby to override the freedom of a scholar to communicate the result of disciplinary investigations.

The case would have been no different if lay administrators of the University of New Hampshire had sought to dictate or determine relevant economic truth and to regulate Paul Sweezy's classroom lectures on that basis.[103] Academic freedom, considered as a constitutional principle, means that a qualified faculty member cannot be reduced to the mouthpiece of non-professional, non-scholarly assessments of relevant knowledge. If a university seeks to censor faculty classroom communications in this way, it becomes, in the words of the *1915 Declaration*, an "essentially proprietary" institution[104] dedicated to promulgating particular views rather than to sustaining the ongoing scholarly discipline by which knowledge is identified and expanded.

As Dewey observed at the outset of the last century, the purpose of such a sham university would be to perpetuate "a certain way of looking at things current among a given body of persons. . . . to disciple rather than to discipline."[105] True universities that protect academic freedom, and that are accordingly entitled to claim the protection of academic freedom, are instead dedicated to the disciplinary diffusion of knowledge and to the disciplinary discovery of new knowledge. It is only in such circumstances that universities serve the constitutional value of democratic competence. It follows that First Amendment coverage should be triggered whenever the publication of research in the classroom is inhibited for reasons that do not depend upon ensuring disciplinary competence as determined by disciplinary experts.

The Court has recently rendered a decision that potentially takes a long step toward entrenching a constitutional vision of universities that disciple rather than discipline. In *Garcetti v. Ceballos*[106] the Court held "that when public employees make statements pursuant to their official duties, the employees are not speaking as citizens for First Amendment purposes, and the Constitution does not insulate their communications from employer discipline."[107] In the context of secondary schools, *Garcetti* has been interpreted to deny all academic freedom in the classroom because a "school system does not 'regulate' teachers' speech as much as it *hires* that speech. Expression is a teacher's stock in trade, the commodity she sells to her employer in exchange for a salary."[108]

In the context of public universities, some courts have interpreted *Garcetti* to mean that "[i]n order for a public employee to raise a successful First Amendment claim, he must have spoken in his capacity as a private citizen and not as an employee."[109] Because faculty communicate in a classroom in their capacity as employees, this conclusion threatens to strip classroom communications of academic freedom protections. The idea is apparently that public universities are proprietary institutions which hire faculty in order to communicate a proprietary message. Aware that its holding might have drastic implications for academic freedom of research, the Court in *Garcetti* notes that "[t]here is some argument that expression related to academic scholarship or classroom instruction implicates additional constitutional interests that are not fully accounted for by this Court's customary employee-speech jurisprudence," and it concludes that "[w]e need not, and for that reason do not, decide whether the analysis we conduct today would apply in the same manner to a case involving speech related to scholarship or teaching."[110]

It is precisely to avoid the logic implicit in *Garcetti* that the drafters of the *1915 Declaration* insisted that faculty "are the appointees, but not in any proper sense the employees," of universities.[111]

> [O]nce appointed, the scholar has professional functions to perform in which the appointing authorities have neither competency nor moral right to intervene. The responsibility of the university teacher is primarily to the public itself, and to his judgment of his own profession; and, while, with respect to certain external conditions of his vocation, he accepts a responsibility to the authorities of the institution in which he serves, in the essentials of his professional activity his duty is to the wider public to which the institution itself is morally amenable. So far as the university

teacher's independence of thought and utterance is concerned—though not in other regards—the relationship of professor to trustees may be compared to that between judges of the federal courts and the executive who appoints them. University teachers should be understood to be, with respect to the conclusions reached and expressed by them, no more subject to the control of the trustees, than are the judges subject to the control of the president, with respect to their decisions; while of course, for the same reason, trustees are no more to be held responsible for, or to be presumed to agree with, the opinions or utterances of professors, than the president can be assumed to approve of the legal reasonings of the courts.[112]

Translated into contemporary constitutional terms, the argument of the *Declaration* is that faculty serve the "public" insofar as they serve the public function of identifying and discovering knowledge. It is this function that triggers the constitutional value of democratic competence. Were faculty to be merely employees of a university, as *Garcetti* conceptualizes employees, their job would be to transmit the views of university administrators. Faculty would then no longer expand knowledge, because they would no longer be responsible for applying independent professional, disciplinary standards. In such circumstances, universities would no longer advance the value of democratic competence.

This is a dire result. It would strip this nation of an invaluable resource, one that has propelled us to the forefront of the world stage. In today's information age, intellectual stagnation implies economic and military failure. Much depends, therefore, on the extent to which the Court appreciates the full weight that rides on the casual reservation that it advanced in *Garcetti*.

Conclusion

At the very outset of the modern age, Francis Bacon grasped that "knowledge it selfe is a power."[1] There is "no doubt," Bacon concluded, but "the sovereignty of Man lieth hid in knowledge."[2] Our own democratic era has drawn an important implication from Bacon's insight. A people without knowledge is a people without power or sovereignty. To preserve the self-government of the people, we must preserve their access to knowledge. We must safeguard their democratic competence.

T. S. Eliot famously lamented,

Where is the wisdom we have lost in knowledge?
Where is the knowledge we have lost in information?[3]

Knowledge, particularly the kind of expert knowledge we have been discussing in this book, is synonymous neither with wisdom nor with information. Expert knowledge is neither practical reason nor is it a collection of atomistic facts. Expert knowledge arises from the capacity to arrange experience in dependable and useful ways. It is produced through the application of complex disciplinary practices.

From this simple proposition follows the radical and counterintuitive conclusion that democratic competence can be constitutionally protected only if the disciplinary practices that create expert knowledge are themselves invested with constitutional status. If we closely scrutinize contemporary First Amendment doctrine, we can discern a faint but distinct tendency to do just this. The most obvious example is the constitutional protection accorded academic freedom. Yet the lamentable disarray of judicial precedents regarding academic freedom illustrates how inchoate and untheorized is our present understanding of the constitutional value of democratic competence.

If courts were more self-consciously and systematically to recognize the constitutional value of democratic competence, they would require criteria to determine *which* disciplinary practices implicate the value and which do not. The practices of astrology and palmistry would not qualify, but those of chemistry, law, and medicine probably would. As courts pursue these distinctions, they will necessarily enact a constitutional sociology of knowledge. Disciplines that are regarded as contributing to the value of democratic competence will receive First Amendment *coverage,* as distinct from First Amendment *protection.*[4] In practice, this implies that attempted regulation of such disciplines will raise First Amendment issues that must be resolved by distinctive First Amendment doctrinal tests.

There may be circumstances when disciplinary experts stand firmly united against state efforts to regulate knowledge. Recent examples include statutes enacted by South Dakota and Nebraska requiring doctors to convey misinformation to patients.[5] In such circumstances, government attempts to suppress disciplinary expertise are easily exposed as purely ideological. Inchoate First Amendment instincts to protect democratic competence are fully aroused.

Healthy disciplines, however, are frequently sites of controversy. Disciplines grow and develop because they encompass a vibrant "place for criticism and critical transformation" at their "heart."[6] If a state intervenes in intra-disciplinary controversies to enforce the views of some members of a discipline against the views of others within the same discipline, it may be difficult for a court to determine whether the value of democratic competence is truly at stake. The more divided the community of disciplinary expertise, the greater the leeway for political control. A state seeking to suppress medical advice as malpractice will be in a constitutionally vulnerable position if it seeks to override the unanimous opinion of medical experts; to the extent that the state can claim to rely on the opinion of credible medical experts, the strength of its constitutional position will increase.

There are often very good reasons to control the communication of expert opinion. Like all human institutions, knowledge-creating professions and disciplines have their own dynamics of power.[7] They are not neutral and disinterested, whatever that may mean. Government may properly seek to regulate professional disciplinary speech whenever experts resist needed change out of inertia or self-interest, or whenever political control is required to render professions responsive to contemporary needs and values.[8] Political correction may at times be necessary to overcome the temptation of professional experts to engage in forms self-aggrandizement that harm the public.

Extending First Amendment coverage to such situations does not imply that state regulations of disciplinary speech are inherently unconstitutional. It merely recognizes that such regulations pose the potential danger of government control over the construction of knowledge. Extending First Amendment coverage to such situations therefore puts the state to its proof whenever it seeks to manipulate the creation and diffusion of disciplinary knowledge.

Balancing the need for political control against the danger of state overreaching entails the same delicate juggling that underwrites all liberal efforts to create dynamic systems of checks and balances. There is no general theoretical solution for attaining the right balance; there is only an endless process of adjustment. As Anthony Giddens remarks, "[T]here is no alternative to the rule of science and expertise,"[9] and yet "the intrusion of the lay public, organizations and states into contexts which scientists themselves might like to claim as 'autonomous'" raises "issues of a complicated kind."[10] The issues are "complicated" because they span irresolvable tensions.

It is of some constitutional importance to maintain these tensions. Precisely because standard First Amendment jurisprudence prizes opinion, and indeed precisely because it tends to reduce complex speech to opinions that can be neither true nor false, standard First Amendment jurisprudence virtually invites the state to suppress knowledge practices to serve short-term political and ideological interests. Yet such suppression potentially endangers the constitutional value of democratic competence. By maintaining a continuous tension between state authority to regulate expert knowledge practices on the one hand, and the relative constitutional autonomy of such knowledge practices on the other, we recognize and honor the need to negotiate between these two important social needs.

Notes

Introduction

1. Davenport v. Washington Educ. Ass'n., 551 U.S. 177, 188–89 (2007).
2. 250 U.S. 616 (1919).
3. Robert Post, *Reconciling Theory and Doctrine in First Amendment Jurisprudence*, 88 CALIF. L. REV. 2355, 2359 (2000).
4. *Abrams*, 250 U.S. at 630 (Holmes, J., dissenting).
5. Red Lion Broad. v. FCC, 395 U.S. 367, 390 (1969).
6. Gloria Franke, *The Right of Publicity vs. The First Amendment: Will One Test Ever Capture the Starring Role?*, 79 S. Cal. L. Rev. 945, 958 (2006).
7. *See, e.g.*, S. Brannon Latimer, *Can Felon Disenfranchisement Survive Under Modern Conceptions of Voting Rights?: Political Philosophy, State Interests, and Scholarly Scorn*, 59 SMU L. Rev. 1841, 1862 (2006) (A central purpose of the First Amendment is that of "'advancing knowledge' and 'truth' in the 'marketplace of ideas'").
8. William P. Marshall, *In Defense of the Search for Truth as a First Amendment Justification*, 30 GA. L. REV. 1, 1 (1995).
9. For classic analysis, see C. EDWIN BAKER, HUMAN LIBERTY AND FREEDOM OF SPEECH 6–46 (1989). *See also* Edwin Baker, *First Amendment Limits on Copyright*, 55 VAND. L. REV. 891, 897 (2002) (The "marketplace of ideas theory is fundamentally unsound both normatively and descriptively."); FREDERICK SCHAUER, FREE SPEECH: A PHILOSOPHICAL ENQUIRY 15–34 (1982); David A. Strauss, *Persuasion, Autonomy, and Freedom of Expression*, 91 COLUM. L. REV. 334, 348–50 (1991); Stanley Ingber, *The Marketplace of Ideas: A Legitimizing Myth*, 1984 DUKE L.J. 1. In the light

of these notorious objections, Vince Blasi has offered a fundamental reinterpretation of the value expressed in Holmes's metaphor of the marketplace of ideas:

> As Holmes understood the notion, the marketplace of ideas does not offer the prospect of a just distribution of the opportunity to persuade. It does not offer the prospect of wisdom through mass deliberation, nor that of meaningful political participation for all interested citizens. What the marketplace of ideas does offer is a much needed counterweight, both conceptual and rhetorical, to illiberal attitudes about authority and change on which the censorial mentality thrives. It honors certain character traits—inquisitiveness, capacity to admit error and to learn from experience, ingenuity, willingness to experiment, resilience—that matter in civic adaptation no less than economic. It devalues deference and discredits certitude, and in the process holds various forms of incumbent authority accountable to standards of performance. It offers a reason to interpret the First Amendment to protect some gestures of opposition and resistance that have nothing to do with dialogue or dialectic.

Vincent Blasi, *Holmes and the Marketplace of Ideas,* 2004 SUP. CT. REV. 1, 45–46 (2004).

10. *See* Robert Post, *Debating Disciplinarity,* 35 CRITICAL INQUIRY 749 (2009).

11. *See, e.g.,* Richard Lewontin, *Billions and Billions of Demons,* N.Y. REV. BOOKS, Jan. 9, 1997, at 28. ("[G]iven the immense extent, inherent complexity, and counterintuitive nature of scientific knowledge, it is impossible for anyone, including non-specialist scientists, to retrace the intellectual paths that lead to scientific conclusions about nature. In the end we must trust the experts and they, in turn, exploit their authority as experts and their rhetorical skills to secure our attention and our belief in things that we do not really understand."). As Anthony Giddens writes,

> By expert systems I mean systems of technical accomplishment or professional expertise that organize large areas of the

material and social environments in which we live today. Most laypersons consult "professionals"—lawyers, architects, doctors, and so forth—only in a periodic or irregular fashion. But the systems in which the knowledge of experts is integrated influence many aspects of what we do in a *continuous* way. . . . I know very little about the codes of knowledge used by the architect and the builder in the design and construction of the home, but I nonetheless have "faith" in what they have done. My "faith" is not so much in them . . . as in the authenticity of the expert knowledge which they apply— something which I cannot usually check exhaustively myself.

ANTHONY GIDDENS, THE CONSEQUENCES OF MODERNITY 27–28 (1990).

12. "The institutional structure of scholarly journals serves to reinforce disciplinary hierarchies: at the lowest level, the evaluator, reader, or reviewer is implicitly considered to be qualified to make judgments about a contribution at a level above that of the contributor himself. From there the hierarchy extends to the editorship, and the selection processes for filling the intervening positions evidently reinforce the hierarchizing and orthodoxy of the discipline in question." Wolfram W. Swoboda, *Disciplines and Interdisciplinarity: A Historical Perspective, in* INTERDISCIPLINARITY IN HIGHER EDUCATION 49, 78–99 (Joseph J. Kockelmans ed. 1979). See Ellen Messer-Davidow, *Book Review,* 17 SIGNS at 676, 679: "Gatekeepers, by virtue of their position as evaluators (editors of journals, referees of manuscripts, reviewers of grant proposals), decide which work will be presented in public forums and which will languish in obscurity. Upon cumulative decisions of this kind depend the professional and epistemological selections—who gets tenured and promoted, which knowledges are advanced and disseminated—that constitute a disciplinary repertoire."

13. CHARLES PEIRCE, *The Fixation of Belief, in* VALUES IN A UNIVERSE OF CHANCE 91, 110–11 (Philip P. Wiener ed., 1958). Of course, as Susan Haack properly observes:

There is no algorithmic "scientific method," no formal, or formalizable, procedure available to all scientists and only to scientists, which, faithfully followed, guarantees success, or even progress. But over centuries of work, scientists have gradually developed a vast array of special tools and techniques, ever more-powerful instruments of observation, ever more-cunning (and sometimes very formally precise) experimental designs, ever more-sophisticated mathematical and statistical techniques, ever fancier computer programs, and so on. These scientific "helps" to inquiry usually develop in an ad hoc way, in response to some problem at hand; and almost always they rely on some earlier scientific innovation, theoretical or practical. The evolution of such "technical" helps to inquiry has been an untidy, pragmatic, fallible, bootstrap process that has gradually made it possible to get more and better-focused evidence and to assess more accurately where evidence leads—in short, to extend and amplify unaided human cognitive powers.

Susan Haack, *Irreconcilable Differences? The Troubled Marriage of Science and Law*, 72 LAW & CONTEMP. PROBS. Winter 2009, at 1, 8–9.

1
Democratic Legitimation and the First Amendment

1. Frederick Schauer, *Categories and the First Amendment: A Play in Three Acts*, 34 VAND. L. REV. 265, 267 (1981).
2. Glickman v. Wileman Bros. & Elliott, Inc., 521 U.S. 457, 478 (1997) (Souter, J., dissenting) (emphasis added). *See, e.g.,* Barry P. McDonald, *Government Regulation or Other "Abridgments" of Scientific Research: The Proper Scope of Judicial Review Under the First Amendment*, 54 EMORY L.J. 979, 1009 (2005) ("[A]ll speech receives First Amendment protection unless it falls within certain narrow categories of expression that are of 'such slight social value as a step to truth that any benefit that may be derived from them is clearly outweighed by the social interest in order and morality'— such as incitement of imminent illegal conduct, intentional libel, obscenity, child pornography, fighting words, and true threats.").

Throughout the history of First Amendment theory, this view has been known as the "two-level theory" of First Amendment coverage. *See* Nat Stern, *The Doubtful Validity of Victim-Specific Libel Laws,* 52 Vill. L. Rev. 533, 534–35 (2005); Tom Hentoff, *Speech, Harm, and Self-Government: Understanding the Ambit of the Clear and Present Danger Test,* 91 Colum. L. Rev. 1453, 1462–63 (1991); Harry Kalven, Jr., *The Metaphysics of the Law of Obscenity,* 1960 Sup. Ct. Rev. 1, 10–12 (1960).

3. Thomas I. Emerson, The System of Freedom of Expression 8–9 (1970).

4. *Id.* at 8.

5. 418 U.S. 405, 410–11 (1974).

6. "[O]ne cannot burn down someone's house to make a political point and then seek refuge in the First Amendment." Virginia v. Black, 538 U.S. 343, 394 (2003) (Thomas, J., dissenting).

7. *On Liars, in* Michel de Montaigne, Essays 31 (J.M. Cohen, trans., 1958).

8. Joseph Burstyn, Inc. v. Wilson, 343 U.S. 495, 501 (1952).

9. Hurley v. Irish-American Gay, Lesbian and Bisexual Group, 515 U.S. 557 (1995).

10. *Id.* at 569. For a full discussion, see Robert Post, *Recuperating First Amendment Doctrine,* 47 Stan. L. Rev. 1249 (1995).

11. Hence Wittgenstein's famous pronouncement: "Words are deeds." Ludwig Wittgenstein, Culture and Value ¶ 46e (P. Winch trans., 1980).

12. Consider, for example, Emerson's discussion of espionage:

> Perhaps a word should be added concerning the classification of espionage as "action." It is true that espionage usually involves the communication of information, and this by itself would normally be considered "expression." But espionage does take place in a context of action; the espionage apparatus is engaged primarily in conduct that dwarfs any element of expression.

Emerson, *supra* note 3, at 58. The passage amounts to a concession that First Amendment coverage cannot be defined in terms of the communication of ideas.

13. *Id.* at 18. Edwin Baker offers a similar interpretation of Emerson in C. EDWIN BAKER, HUMAN LIBERTY AND FREEDOM OF SPEECH 70–73 (1989).

14. Of course, the scope of First Amendment coverage will change as these purposes change.

15. *See* Robert Post, *Reconciling Theory and Doctrine in First Amendment Jurisprudence,* 88 CALIF. L. REV. (2000). For a discussion of the First Amendment in the years before 1919, *see* DAVID M. RABBAN, FREE SPEECH IN ITS FORGOTTEN YEARS (1997). In 1833 the eminent commentator Joseph Story opined "that the language of this amendment imports no more, than that every man shall have a right to speak, write, and print his opinions upon any subject whatsoever, without any prior restraint, so always, that he does not injure any other person in his rights, person, property, or reputation; and so always that he does not thereby disturb the public peace, or attempt to subvert the government." JOSEPH STORY, 3 COMMENTARIES ON THE CONSTITUTION OF THE UNITED STATES 732 (1833).

> That this amendment was intended to secure to every citizen an absolute right to speak, or write, or print, whatever he might please, without any responsibility, public or private . . . is a supposition too wild to be indulged by any rational man. This would be to allow to every citizen a right to destroy, at his pleasure, the reputation, the peace, the property, and even the personal safety of every other citizen.

Id. at 731–32. Story acknowledged, however, that his views were controverted. *Id.* at 738–44.

16. JOHN RAWLS, A THEORY OF JUSTICE 46–49 (1971).

17. Hanna Fenichel Pitkin, *The Idea of a Constitution,* 37 J. LEG. EDUC. 167, 169 (1987).

18. EMERSON, *supra* note 3, at 6. Because Emerson sought to build his First Amendment theory on the distinction between speech and action, he was eclectic and comprehensive in the "values and functions" that he thought the First Amendment would serve. *Id.*

19. *Id.*

20. This theory is most prominently associated with ALEXANDER MEI-

KLEJOHN, POLITICAL FREEDOM: THE CONSTITUTIONAL POWERS OF THE PEOPLE (1965).

21. Immanuel Kant, *An Answer to the Question, What Is Enlightening?*, *in* I ESSAYS AND TREATISES ON MORAL, POLITICAL, AND VARIOUS PHILOSOPHICAL SUBJECTS 3 (1798–99).

22. MICHAEL WILLIAMS, PROBLEMS OF KNOWLEDGE: A CRITICAL INTRODUCTION TO EPISTEMOLOGY 17 (2001).

23. ALLAN GIBBARD, THINKING HOW TO LIVE 226 (2003).

24. *Id.* at 227.

25. *Id.*

26. CASS R. SUNSTEIN, INFOTOPIA: HOW MANY MINDS PRODUCE KNOWLEDGE 9, 16 (2006). *See* JAMES SUROWIECKI, THE WISDOM OF CROWDS: WHY THE MANY ARE SMARTER THAN THE FEW AND HOW COLLECTIVE WISDOM SHAPES WISDOM, ECONOMIES, SOCIETIES AND NATIONS (2004).

27. SUNSTEIN, *supra* note 26, at 217.

28. *Id.* at 15–16.

29. For a good discussion, see Christopher P. Guzelian, *Scientific Speech,* 93 IOWA L. REV. 881, 892 n.41 (2008).

30. *Wikipedia: No Original Research,* WIKIPEDIA, http://en.wikipedia .org/wiki/Wikipedia:No_original_research.

31. *Wikipedia: Verifiability,* WIKIPEDIA, http://en.wikipedia.org/wiki/ Wikipedia:Verifiability.

32. *Wikipedia: Reliable Sources,* WIKIPEDIA, http://en.wikipedia.org/ wiki/Wikipedia:Reliable_sources. ("Material that has been vetted by the scholarly community is regarded as reliable; this means published in reputable peer-reviewed sources and/or by well-regarded academic presses.").

33. *See* BERNARD WILLIAMS, TRUTH AND TRUTHFULNESS: AN ESSAY IN GENEALOGY 213–19 (2002).

34. Perhaps Charles Sanders Peirce said it best:

> Some persons fancy that bias and counter-bias are favorable to the extraction of truth—that hot and partisan debate is the way to investigate. This is the theory of our atrocious legal procedure. But Logic puts its heel upon this suggestion. It irrefragably demonstrates that knowledge can only be

furthered by the real desire for it, and that the methods of obstinacy, of authority, and every mode of trying to reach a foregone conclusion, are absolutely of no value. These things are proved. The reader is at liberty to think so or not as long as the proof is not set forth, or as long as he refrains from examining it. Just so, he can preserve, if he likes, his freedom of opinion in regard to the propositions of geometry; only, in that case, if he takes a fancy to read Euclid, he will do well to skip whatever he finds with A, B, C, etc., for, if he reads attentively that disagreeable matter, the freedom of his opinion about geometry may unhappily be lost forever.

CHARLES SANDERS PEIRCE, 2 COLLECTED PAPERS 635 (Charles Hartshorne, Paul Weiss, and Arthur Burks eds. Cambridge, MA: Harvard University Press, 1931–58).

35. Rule 702 provides: "If scientific, technical, or other specialized knowledge will assist the trier of fact to understand the evidence or to determine a fact in issue, a witness qualified as an expert by knowledge, skill, experience, training, or education, may testify thereto in the form of an opinion or otherwise."

36. Weisgram v. Marley Co., 528 U.S. 440, 455 (2000).

37. Daubert v. Merrell Dow Pharmaceuticals, Inc., 509 U.S. 579, 592–93 (1993).

38. *Id.* at 593. In *Kumho Tire Co. v. Carmichael,* 526 U.S. 137 (1999), the Court held that this standard applies to all expert testimony based upon technical knowledge, not just to "scientific" knowledge. *Id.* at 147. *See* Alvin I. Goldman, *Experts: Which Ones Should You Trust?,* 63 PHIL. & PHENOMENOLOGICAL RES. 85 (2001). Goldman writes that "[t]he admission of testimony by experts (Rule 702) . . . exemplifies a dedication to truth, since experts are people presumed to know relevant truths." Alvin I. Goldman, *Epistemic Paternalism: Communication Control in Law and Society,* 99 J. PHIL. 113, 115 (1991). On the relationship between disciplinary practices and the production of knowledge for the administrative state, see Patrick A. Fuller, *How Peer Review of Agency Science Can Help Rulemaking: Enhancing Judicial Deference at the Frontiers of Knowledge,* 75 GEO. WASH. L. REV. 931 (2007).

39. Rosenberger v. Rector & Visitors of the Univ. of Va., 515 U.S. 819, 834 (1995).
40. Turner Broad. Sys., Inc. v. FCC, 512 U.S. 622, 642 (1994).
41. Steven J. Heyman, *Spheres of Autonomy: Reforming the Content Neutrality Doctrine in First Amendment Jurisprudence,* 10 WM. & MARY BILL RTS. J. 647, 650 (2002); Paul Horwitz, *Universities as First Amendment Institutions: Some Easy Answers and Hard Questions,* 54 UCLA L. REV. 1497, 1506 (2007).
42. Nevada Comm'n on Ethics v. Carrigan, 131 S. Ct. 2343, 2347 (2011). "If there is a bedrock principle underlying the First Amendment, it is that the government may not prohibit the expression of an idea simply because society finds the idea itself offensive or disagreeable." *Texas v. Johnson,* 491 U.S. 397, 414 (1989).
43. Hustler Magazine, Inc. v. Falwell, 485 U.S. 46, 51 (1988).
44. Explaining the falsity of the proposition that "more total truth possession will be achieved if speech is regulated only by free-market mechanisms rather than by other forms of regulation," the social epistemologist Alvin Goldman has observed:

> Domains of opinions where speech is totally unregulated, or is at most regulated by the market, are arguably the domains where maximum error and falsity are to be found. We have in mind domains in which rumor, gossip, old-wives' tales, and superstition flourish, where astrology and the occult are purveyed and apparently believed. . . . Formal education is highly regulated: Teachers are selected for their training and comparative expertise, and not everyone is allowed to teach in the classroom. Nor is such regulation simply a matter of the market; public education, at any rate, seems to be a nonmarket enterprise. . . .
>
> Next, consider certain forums for scientific and scholarly speech that are highly regulated, and which, nonetheless, are responsible for what many people take to be the greatest amount of knowledge. Scientific, professional, and academic journals are widely thought (certainly by scientists and academics) to be the best forums available for discovering and learning truths, yet these communications systems are highly

regulated. Editors and referees impose stringent criteria for the publication of submitted manuscripts. Attempts to "speak" in these forums are often rigidly controlled. People lacking the methodologies and technical skills demanded by these journals have no chance of getting their thoughts aired therein, and even well-trained practitioners encounter difficulties. But regulated journals of this sort are widely thought to be effective in promoting truth.

Alvin I. Goldman, *Speech, Truth, and the Free Market for Ideas*, 2 LEGAL THEORY 1, 4, 12–13 (1996).

45. MEIKLEJOHN, *supra* note 20, at 27.

46. *See, e.g.*, Bd. of Airport Comm'rs of Los Angeles v. Jews for Jesus, 482 U.S. 569 (1987); Stanley v. Georgia, 394 U.S. 557 (1969).

47. For a summary, see Robert Post, *The Constitutional Concept of Public Discourse: Outrageous Opinion, Democratic Deliberation, and Hustler Magazine v. Falwell*, 103 HARV. L. REV. 601, 667–68 (1990).

48. New York Times Co. v. Sullivan, 376 U.S. 254, 269–70 (1964) (quoting Roth v. United States, 354 U.S. 476, 484 (1957)).

49. Dun & Bradstreet, Inc. v. Greenmoss Builders, Inc., 472 U.S. 749, 758–59 (1985) (plurality opinion); *see* Philadelphia Newspapers, Inc. v. Hepps, 475 U.S. 767 , 775 (1986).

50. Dombey v. Phoenix Newspapers, Inc., 724 P.2d 562, 567 (Ariz. 1986). *See* Noonan v. Staples, Inc., 556 F.3d 20, 25–26 (1st Cir. 2009); Mutafis v. Erie Ins. Exch., 775 F.2d 593, 594–95 (4th Cir. 1985) (per curiam); Ramirez v. Rogers, 540 A.2d 475, 477–78 (Me. 1988); Cox v. Hatch, 761 P.2d 556, 559 (Utah 1988).

51. Connick v. Myers, 461 U.S. 138, 145 (1983).

52. *See* San Diego v. Roe, 543 U.S. 77 (2004).

53. Garcetti v. Ceballos, 547 U.S. 410, 417 (2006).

54. Snyder v. Phelps, 131 S.Ct. 1207 (2011); Hustler Magazine, Inc. v. Falwell, 485 U.S. 46 (1988).

55. Bartnicki v. Vopper, 532 U.S. 514 (2001).

56. This case is discussed in detail in Robert Post, *Informed Consent to Abortion: A First Amendment Analysis of Compelled Physician Speech*, 2007 ILL. L. REV. 939.

57. Bailey v. Huggins Diagnostic & Rehabilitation Ctr., Inc., 952 P.2d 768, 772 (Colo. Ct. App. 1997).

58. *Id.* at 769.

59. Consider in this regard the famous observation of Justice Jackson that the First Amendment should be interpreted to preserve the "rough distinction" between state rules that seek to suppress the public speech of professionals and therefore should trigger First Amendment coverage, and rules that serve the perfectly routine and constitutionally unobjectionable function of regulating the practice of a profession:

> A state may forbid one without its license to practice law as a vocation, but I think it could not stop an unlicensed person from making a speech about the rights of man or the rights of labor, or any other kind of right, including recommending that his hearers organize to support his views. Likewise, the state may prohibit the pursuit of medicine as an occupation without its license but I do not think it could make it a crime publicly or privately to speak urging persons to follow or reject any school of medical thought. So the state to an extent not necessary now to determine may regulate one who makes a business or a livelihood of soliciting funds or memberships for unions. But I do not think it can prohibit one, even if he is a salaried labor leader, from making an address to a public meeting of workmen, telling them their rights as he sees them and urging them to unite in general or to join a specific union.

Thomas v. Collins, 323 U.S. 516, 544–45 (1945).

60. Thornhill v. Alabama, 310 U.S. 88, 104 (1940).

61. *Id.* at 101–102.

62. Masses Publ'g Co. v. Patten, 244 F. 535, 540 (S.D.N.Y.), *rev'd*, 246 F. 24 (2d Cir. 1917).

63. James Madison, *Public Opinion,* NAT'L GAZETTE, Dec. 19, 1791, *in* 14 JAMES MADISON, THE PAPERS OF JAMES MADISON 170, 170 (Robert A. Rutland et al. eds., 1977).

64. FRANCIS LIEBER, ON CIVIL LIBERTY AND SELF-GOVERNMENT 131 (1859).

65. CARL SCHMITT, CONSTITUTIONAL THEORY 275 (Jeffrey Seitzer trans.

2008). Not only does Schmitt assert that "there is no democracy without public opinion," *id.*, but he also writes that "'People' is a concept that becomes present only in the *public* sphere. The people appear only in the public, and they first produce the public generally. People and public exist together; no people without public and no public without the people." *Id.* at 272.

66. Brown v. Hartlage, 456 U.S. 45, 60 (1982).

67. Cox v. Louisiana, 379 U.S. 559 (1965).

68. Texas v. Johnson, 491 U.S. 397 (1989).

69. Brown v. Louisiana, 383 U.S. 141, 142 (1966) (opinion of Fortas, J.). *See* Garner v. Louisiana, 368 U.S. 157, 201–02 (1961) (opinion of Harlan, J.). On civil disobedience as a traditional American method of opinion formation, see HANNAH ARENDT, CRISES OF THE REPUBLIC 69–102 (1972).

70. *See* Frederick Schauer, *The Boundaries of the First Amendment: A Preliminary Exploration of Constitutional Salience,* 117 HARV. L. REV. 1765 (2004).

71. Rosenberger v. Univ. of Va., 515 U.S. 819, 831 (1995); *see also* Hustler Magazine, Inc. v. Falwell, 485 U.S. 46, 55 (1988).

72. MEIKLEJOHN, *supra* note 20; Robert Bork, *Neutral Principles and Some First Amendment Problems,* 47 IND. L. J. 1 (1971).

73. Bork, *supra* note 72, at 27–28.

74. MEIKLEJOHN, *supra* note 20, at 26.

75. *See, e.g.,* OWEN FISS, LIBERALISM DIVIDED: FREEDOM OF SPEECH AND THE MANY USES OF STATE POWER (1996). For a discussion, see Robert Post, *Equality and Autonomy in First Amendment Jurisprudence,* 95 MICH. L. REV. 1517 (1997).

76. Globe Newspaper Co. v. Superior Court of Norfolk, 457 U.S. 596, 604 (1982) (citing Thornhill v. Alabama, 310 U.S. 88, 95 (1940)).

77. Miller v. California, 413 U.S. 15, 22–23 (1973).

78. I have often heard it argued that because this account of democracy rests on the value of collective autonomy, the protection of individual autonomy must therefore be the most fundamental purpose of the First Amendment. I regard this argument as a non sequitur. All government regulations circumscribe individual autonomy. The First Amendment provides for specialized judicial constraints on particular kinds of otherwise valid state action. We

might well regard the collective autonomy of a well-functioning democracy as sufficient warrant for the limitations on individual autonomy continuously exacted by ordinary government regulation. Conversely, we may regard the distinctive restraints of the First Amendment as necessary to safeguard the very collective autonomy that may immunize ordinary government regulations from routine constitutional scrutiny.

79. I regard the postulate of homogeneity as chimerical. It may be that if all citizens in a state spontaneously agree on government decisions because of some pre-existing cultural homogeneity, democratic legitimacy might be possible without freedom of speech. Rousseau seems to have imagined something like this state of affairs, for he advocated that the general will be formed without public discussion. JEAN-JACQUES ROUSSEAU, THE SOCIAL CONTRACT 73 (Maurice Cranston, trans., 1968). Carl Schmitt also seems to have regarded "the constitutionally unalienated people, in their ethnic and national sameness, as the 'true' foundation of democracy. Democracy is the rule of the people's will, whose essence is collective authenticity; this quality cannot be achieved by mere aggregation of private individual wills; the attribute of elections in liberal democracies. . . . This concept of democratic representation clearly reveals the close connection between democracy and authoritarian rule—an affinity which led Schmitt to the (at a first glance paradoxical) contention that a true dictatorship can only be founded on a democratic basis." Ulrich K. Preuss, *Constitutional Power-making for the New Polity: Some Deliberations on the Relations Between Constituent Power and the Constitution,* 14 CARDOZO L. REV. 639,650–51 (1993). The distinction between democracy and the "true dictatorship" postulated by Schmitt is that the former continuously preserve the space for diversity and dissent, which is assumed always to be present under modern conditions of heterogeneity.

80. JÜRGEN HABERMAS, THE STRUCTURAL TRANSFORMATION OF THE PUBLIC SPHERE 30–31 (Thomas Burger, trans., 1991). The common law privilege of fair comment about matters of public concern, for example, ultimately traces back to an 1808 decision involving the harsh criticism of three travel books. Although the

criticism was otherwise defamatory, the judge charged the jury that:

> Every man who publishes a book commits himself to the judgment of the public, and anyone may comment upon his performance. . . . [W]hatever their merits, others have a right to pass their judgment upon them—to censure them if they be censurable, and to turn them into ridicule if they be ridiculous.

Carr v. Hood, 170 Eng. Rep. 985 n.*, 1 Camp. 357 n.* (K.B. 1808). *See* Hallen, *Fair Comment,* 8 TEX. L. REV. 41, 43–44 (1929).

81. Charles Taylor, *Modern Social Imaginaries,* 14 PUB. CULTURE 91, 112–13 (2002).

82. *Id.* For an excellent discussion of the nature of the public sphere and of its historical emergence, see Charles Taylor, *Liberal Politics and the Public Sphere* in CHARLES TAYLOR, PHILOSOPHICAL ARGUMENTS 257–87 (1995). On the development of the American public sphere, see PAUL STARR, THE CREATION OF THE MEDIA (2004).

83. MICHAEL WARNER, PUBLICS AND COUNTERPUBLICS 11–12 (2002).

84. *Id.* at 68–69. "[A] public can only produce a sense of belonging and activity if it is self-organized through discourse rather than through an external framework. This is why a distortion or blockage in access to a public can be so grave, leading people to feel powerless and frustrated. Externally organized frameworks of activity, such as voting, are and are perceived to be poor substitutes." *Id.* at 70.

85. For a discussion, see Robert Post, *supra* note 10.

86. On this point, see WARNER, *supra* note 83 at 123:

> One of the most striking features of publics, in the modern public sphere, is that they can in some contexts acquire agency. . . . Publics act historically. They are said to rise up, to speak, to reject false promises, to demand answers, to change sovereigns, to support troops, to give mandates for change, to be satisfied, to scrutinize public conduct, to take role models, to deride counterfeits. It is difficult to imagine the modern world without the ability to attribute agency to publics,

though doing so is an extraordinary fiction. It requires us, for example, to understand the ongoing circulatory time of public discourse as though it were discussion leading up to a decision.

The attribution of agency to publics works in most cases because of the direct transposition from private reading acts to the sovereignty of opinion. All of the verbs for public agency are verbs for private reading, transposed upward to the aggregate of readers. Readers may scrutinize, ask, reject, opine, decide, judge, and so on. Publics can do exactly these things. And nothing else. Publics—unlike mobs or crowds— are incapable of any activity that can not be expressed through such a verb. Activities of reading that do not fit the ideology of reading as silent, private, replicable decoding—curling up, mumbling, fantasizing, gesticulating, ventriloquizing, writing marginalia, and so on—also find no counterparts in public agency.

87. JÜRGEN HABERMAS, BETWEEN FACTS AND NORMS: CONTRIBUTIONS TO A DISCOURSE THEORY OF LAW AND DEMOCRACY 486 (William Rehg trans., 1996).

88. Riley v. Nat'l Fed'n of the Blind, 487 U.S. 781, 796–97 (1988).

89. *Id.* at 795.

90. *Id.* at 790–91.

91. *See* Robert Post, *Compelled Subsidization of Speech:* Johanns v. Livestock Marketing Association, 2005 SUP. CT. REV. 195; Robert Post, *Transparent and Efficient Markets: Compelled Commercial Speech and Coerced Commercial Association in* United Foods, Zauderer, *and* Abood, 40 VALP. U. L. REV. 555 (2006).

92. For a discussion, see Robert Post, *Democracy and Equality,* 603 ANNALS AM. ACAD. POL. & SOC. SCI. 24 (2006).

93. *See* Robert Post, *Community and the First Amendment,* 29 ARIZ. ST. L.J. 473 (1997).

94. Compare *supra* note 57 with *Winter v. G.P. Putnam's Sons,* 938 F.2d 1033 (9th Cir. 1991), in which the First Amendment was held to immunize from liability the publisher of the *The Encyclopedia of Mushrooms* in a suit by those who alleged that their health was

gravely damaged by eating poisonous mushrooms in reliance on the information provided by the *Encyclopedia.*

95. Robert Post, *Meiklejohn's Mistake: Individual Autonomy and the Reform of Public Discourse,* 64 Colo. L. Rev. 1109 (1993); Richard H. Fallon, *Two Senses of Autonomy,* 46 Stan. L. Rev. 875 (1994).

96. For examples, see Robert Post, *The Social Foundations of Privacy: Community and Self in the Common Law Tort,* 77 Calif. L. Rev. 957 (1989); Robert Post, *The Social Foundations of Defamation Law: Reputation and the Constitution,* 74 Calif. L. Rev. 691 (1986).

97. The point is theorized in Robert Post, Constitutional Domains: Democracy, Community, Management 1–20 (1995).

98. David R. Shumway & Ellen Messer-Davidow, *Disciplinarity: An Introduction,* Poetics Today Summer 1991 at 201–25, 202.

99. Steven Shapin & Simon Schaffer, Leviathan and the Air-Pump 225 (1989). Shapin and Schaffer argue that the very idea of a "fact" is itself "a constitutively social category" that depends upon conventions that determine how "a private sensory experience is transformed into a publicly witnessed and agreed fact of nature." *Id. See, e.g.,* Catherine Gallagher, *Matters of Fact,* 14 Yale J. L. & Hum. 441 (2002).

100. Karin Knorr Cetina uses the term "epistemic cultures" to refer to "the cultures of knowledge settings" that define "knowledge as practiced—within structures, processes, and environments that make up *specific* epistemic settings." Karen Knorr Cetina: Epistemic Cultures: How the Sciences Make Knowledge 8 (1999). Cetina emphasizes "the machineries of knowing composed of practices." *Id.* at 10.

2

Democratic Competence and the First Amendment

1. Georg Wilhelm Friedrich Hegel, Hegel's Philosophy of Right ¶ 316 (p. 204) (T. M. Knox trans., 1952).

2. *Id.* at ¶ 318 (p. 205).

3. John Stuart Mill, On Liberty 118, 119, 129–30 (The Lawbook Exch., Ltd. 2002) (1859).

4. *Id.* at 13. In the context of the United States, Alexis de Tocqueville

was one of the first to address "that very sore subject, the tyranny of public opinion." John C. Spencer, *Preface to the American Edition* of ALEXIS DE TOCQUEVILLE, DEMOCRACY IN AMERICA at i, v (Henry Reeve, trans., Lawbook Exchange, Ltd. 2003) (1838). De Tocqueville observed that "the public has therefore among a democratic people a singular power, of which aristocratic nations could never so much as conceive an idea; for it does not persuade to certain opinions, but it enforces them, and infuses them into the faculties by a sort of enormous pressure of the minds of all upon the reason of each. In the United States the majority undertakes to supply a multitude of ready-made opinions for the use of individuals, who are thus relieved from the necessity of forming opinions of their own." 2 ALEXIS DE TOCQUEVILLE, DEMOCRACY IN AMERICA 492–93 (Henry Reeve, trans., D. Appleton & Co. 1904) (1838).

5. THOMAS KUHN, THE STRUCTURE OF SCIENTIFIC REVOLUTIONS 168 (2d ed. 1970). See Susan Haack, *Irreconcilable Differences? The Troubled Marriage of Science and Law,* 72 LAW & CONTEMP. PROBS., Winter 2009, at 10. Consider in this regard the facetious editorial that *Scientific American* published on April Fools' Day 2005, *Okay, We Give Up:*

> Good journalism values balance above all else. We owe it to our readers to present everybody's ideas equally and not to ignore or discredit theories simply because they lack scientifically credible arguments or facts. Nor should we succumb to the easy mistake of thinking that scientists understand their fields better than, say, U.S. senators or best-selling novelists do. Indeed, if politicians or special-interest groups say things that seem untrue or misleading, our duty as journalists is to quote them without comment or contradiction. To do otherwise would be elitist and therefore wrong. . . .
>
> Get ready for a new *Scientific American.* . . . This magazine will be dedicated purely to science, fair and balanced science, and not just the science that scientists say is science. And it will start on April Fools' Day.

Sci.Am., April 2005, *available at* http://www.scientificamerican.com/article.cfm?id=okay-we-give-up.

6. *See* Craig Calhoun, *The Promise of Public Sociology*, 56 BRITISH J. SOC. 355, 356–57 (2005) ("Partial autonomy is the condition for transcending the mere play of opinions and clash of powers. A scientific field that did not achieve some capacity for autonomous judgment, that was merely heteronomously controlled by others would not merely lack authority, but lack credibility.").

7. HANNAH ARENDT, BETWEEN PAST AND FUTURE 238 (1968).

8. Gertz v. Robert Welch, Inc., 418 U.S. 323, 340 (1974).

9. *Id.* at 339.

10. No one has analyzed this tension more deeply than Hannah Arendt, who writes that "from the viewpoint of politics, truth has a despotic character," because truth demands acknowledgment regardless of popular debate, whereas "debate constitutes the very essence of political life."

> The modes of thought and communication that deal with truth, if seen from the political perspective, are necessarily domineering; they don't take into account other people's opinions, and taking these into account is the hallmark of all strictly political thinking.
>
> Political thinking is representative. I form an opinion by considering a given issue from different viewpoints, by making present to my mind the standpoints of those who are absent; that is, I represent them. . . . The more people's standpoints I have present in my mind while I am pondering a given issue, and the better I can imagine how I would feel and think if I were in their place, the stronger will be my capacity for representative thinking and the more valid my final conclusions, my opinion.

ARENDT, *supra* note 7 at 241. "Truth," Arendt writes, "carries within itself an element of coercion." *Id.* at 239.

> [H]istorically the conflict between truth and politics arouse out of two diametrically opposed ways of life—the life of the philosopher . . . and the way of life of the citizen. To the citizens' ever-changing opinions about human affairs, which themselves were in a state of constant flux, the philosopher opposed the truth about those things which in their nature

were everlasting and from which, therefore, principles could be derived to stabilize human affairs. Hence the opposite to truth was mere opinion, which was equated with illusion, and it was this degrading of opinion that gave the conflict its political poignancy; for opinion, and not truth, belongs among the indispensable prerequisites of all power. "All governments rest on opinion," James Madison said, and not even the most autocratic ruler or tyrant could ever rise to power, let alone keep it, without the support of those who are likeminded. By the same token, every claim in the sphere of human affairs to an absolute truth, whose validity needs no support from the side of opinion, strikes at the root of all politics and all governments.

Id. at 232–33. Arendt allows us to see that First Amendment protections guarantee the specifically political character of public opinion. To the extent that law enforces claims of truth, it suppresses "political thinking" by excluding from political participation those who embrace a different truth from the state.

11. New York Times Co. v. Sullivan, 376 U.S. 254, 279–80 (1964).
12. *Gertz,* 418 U.S. at 347.
13. *See, e.g., New York Times,* 376 U.S. at 271:

That erroneous statement is inevitable in free debate, and that it must be protected if the freedoms of expression are to have the "breathing space" that they "need * * * to survive," was also recognized by the Court of Appeals for the District of Columbia Circuit in Sweeney v. Patterson. . . . Judge Edgerton spoke for a unanimous court which affirmed the dismissal of a Congressman's libel suit based upon a newspaper article charging him with anti-Semitism in opposing a judicial appointment. He said:

Cases which impose liability for erroneous reports of the political conduct of officials reflect the obsolete doctrine that the governed must not criticize their governors. * * * The interest of the public here outweighs the interest of appellant or any other individual. The protection of the public requires not merely discussion, but information.

> Political conduct and views which some respectable people approve, and others condemn, are constantly imputed to Congressmen. Errors of fact, particularly in regard to a man's mental states and processes, are inevitable. * * * Whatever is added to the field of libel is taken from the field of free debate.

The basic insight is that the "First Amendment requires that we protect some falsehood in order to protect speech that matters." *Gertz*, 418 U.S. at 341.

14. Moldea v. New York Times Co., 22 F.3d 310, 317 (D.C. Cir.), *cert. denied*, 513 U.S. 875 (1994) (quoting Liberty Lobby, Inc. v. Dow Jones & Co., 838 F.2d 1287, 1292 (D.C. Cir.) (citing Philadelphia Newspapers, Inc. v. Hepps, 475 U.S. 767, 776 (1986), *cert. denied* 486 U.S. 825 (1988))). For accounts of the fact/opinion distinction, see Robert Post, *The Constitutional Concept of Public Discourse: Outrageous Opinion, Democratic Deliberation, and Hustler Magazine v. Falwell*, 103 HARV. L. REV., 601, 649–67 (1990); Robert D. Sack, *Protection of Opinion Under the First Amendment: Reflections on Alfred Hill, 'Defamation and Privacy Under the First Amendment,'* 100 COLUM. L. REV. 294 (2000); Kathryn Dix Sowle, *A Matter of Opinion: Milkovich Four Years Later*, 3 WM. & MARY BILL RTS J. 467 (1994).

15. Ollman v. Evans, 750 F.2d 970, 978 (D.C. Cir. 1984) (en banc), *cert. denied*, 471 U.S. 1127 (1985).

16. Haynes v. Alfred A. Knopf, 8 F.3d 1222, 1227 (7th Cir. 1993). *See* Gray v. St. Martin's Press, Inc., 221 F.3d 243, 248 (1st Cir. 2000), *cert. denied*, 531 U.S. 1075 (2001).

17. Underwager v. Salter, 22 F.3d 730, 735–36 (7th Cir. 1994), *cert. denied*, 513 U.S. 943 (1994).

18. *Id.* "Judges," it is said, "are not well equipped to resolve academic controversies." Dilworth v. Dudley, 75 F.3d 307, 310 (7th Cir. 1996). *See* Oxycal Lab., Inc. v. Jeffers, 909 F.Supp. 719, 724 (S.D. Cal. 1995) ("The Court cannot inquire into the validity of . . . scientific theories, nor should it.").

19. Metabolife Int'l, Inc. v. Wornick, 72 F.Supp.2d 1160, 1172 (S.D. Cal. 1999), *aff'd in part and rev'd in part*, 264 F.3d 832 (9th Cir.

2001). *See* Ezrailson v. Rohrich, 65 S.W. 3d 373, 382 (Tex. App. 2001):

> Scientists continuously call into question and test hypotheses and theories; this questioning advances knowledge. . . . If advancement in medical scientific knowledge is essential to society, "inquiries into these problems, speculations about them, stimulation in others of reflection upon them, must be left as unfettered as possible." . . .
>
> In making the threshold determination of whether a medical science article is reasonably capable of defamatory meaning in light of surrounding circumstances, we believe a court should weigh the need to protect intellectual reputation against society's great need to permit an unfettered discussion of medical science hypotheses. Certainly statements are not immune from the control of defamation law merely because they appear in medical science articles. However, in the area of medical science research, criticism of the creative research ideas of other medical scientists should not be restrained by fear of a defamation claim in the event the criticism itself also ultimately fails for lack of merit. We believe calling the medical science research article here defamatory would serve to unduly restrict the free flow of ideas essential to medical science discourse.

> *See* Michael Kent Curtis, *Monkey Trials: Science, Defamation, and the Suppression of Dissent,* 4 WM. & MARY BILL RTS J. 507, 593 (1995) ("By deciding the falsity of hypotheses, a court 'could preempt future scientific inquiry.'").

20. MICHAEL WALZER, THINKING POLITICALLY: ESSAYS IN POLITICAL THEORY 19 (2007). Discussing Plato's idea of the "tyranny of truth," Arendt puts the point this way:

> As soon as the philosopher submitted his truth, the reflection of the eternal, to the polis, it became immediately an opinion among opinions. It lost its distinguishing quality, for there is no visible hallmark which marks off truth from opinion. It is

as though the moment the eternal is brought into the midst of men it becomes temporal, so that the very discussion of it with others already threatens the existence of the realm in which the lovers of wisdom move.

Hannah Arendt, *Philosophy and Politics,* 57 Soc. Res. 73, 78–79.

21. Allen Buchanan, *Political Liberalism and Social Epistemology,* 32 Phil. & Pub. Aff. 95, 99 (2004).

22. *Id.* at 103.

23. *Id.* at 118.

24. John Dewey, The Public and Its Problems 177–79 (1927). "Unless there are methods . . . what passes as public opinion will be 'opinion' in its derogatory sense rather than truly public, no matter how widespread the opinion is." *Id.* at 177.

25. *See* E. W. Caspari & R. E. Marshak, *The Rise and Fall of Lysenko,* 149 Sci. 275, 275 (1965) (noting that "[n]ot only does the decline in the fortunes of Lysenko reflect the continuing improvement in the scientific climate in the U.S.S.R. . . . , but his career is an object lesson on the harm which results from an attempt to impose an external dogmatism on science"); *see also* S. M. Gershenson, *Difficult Years in Soviet Genetics,* 65 Q. Rev. Biology 447, 447 (1990); Howard Simons, *Russian Genetics and Chickens,* 73 Sci. Newsl. 298, 298 (1958).

26. Ron Suskind, *Without a Doubt,* N.Y. Times Mag., October 17, 2004, at 51 (quoting one senior adviser to Bush to the effect that "When we act, we create our own reality. And while you're studying that reality—judiciously, as you will—we'll act again, creating other new realities, which you can study too. . . . We're history's actors . . . and you, all of you, will be left to just study what we do."). On the potentially dire consequences of acting in this way, see, for example, Juliet Eilperin, *Climate Findings Were Distorted, Probe Finds; Appointees in NASA Press Office Blamed,* Wash. Post, June 3, 2008, at A-02 ("An investigation by the NASA inspector general found that political appointees in the space agency's public affairs office worked to control and distort public accounts of its researchers' findings about climate change for at least two years"); John Johnson Jr., *Bush Appointee Steps Down from Post at NASA,*

L.A. TIMES, February 9, 2006, at A-16 (NASA public affairs official George C. Deutsch was accused of exerting political pressure on agency scientists, "ordering that the word 'theory' be added after every mention of the big bang, which proposes that the universe began with a gigantic explosion. . . . Deutsch wrote that the big bang was 'not proven fact; it is opinion.'"); Lawrence K. Altman, *Panel Finds No Connection Between Cancer and Abortion*, N.Y. TIMES, March 7, 2003, at A-22 ("A scientific panel appointed by the director of the National Cancer Institute has concluded that there is no evidence that having an abortion increases the risk of breast cancer later in life, a suggestion raised earlier on the agency's Web site. Critics have contended that the Bush administration revised its fact sheets on the connection between induced abortions and breast cancer to satisfy conservative constituents, a charge that administration officials have rejected.").

27. CLAUDE LEFORT, DEMOCRACY AND POLITICAL THEORY 15 (David Macey trans., 1988).

28. The insight is a common one. *See, e.g.,* GEORGE ORWELL, 3 THE COLLECTED ESSAYS, JOURNALISM, AND LETTERS OF GEORGE ORWELL: As I PLEASE, 1943–1945, at 87–89 (Sonia Orwell and Ian Angus eds. 2000) ("The really frightening thing about totalitarianism is not that it commits 'atrocities' but that it attacks the concept of objective truth; it claims to control the past as well as the future.").

29. KAREN KNORR CETINA: EPISTEMIC CULTURES: HOW THE SCIENCES MAKE KNOWLEDGE 5 (1999); *see* Nikolas Rose and Peter Miller, *Political Power Beyond the State: Problematics of Government,* 43 BRIT. J. SOC. 173, 175 (1992) ("Knowledge is . . . central to [the] activities of government and to the very formation of its objects, for government is a domain of cognition, calculation, experimentation and evaluation.").

30. *See, e.g.,* Dorothy E. Roberts, Rust v. Sullivan *and the Control of Knowledge,* 61 GEO. WASH. L. REV. 587 (1993).

31. Jeremy Bentham, *Essay on Political Tactics, in* 2 THE WORKS OF JEREMY BENTHAM 312 (John Bowring ed., 1843).

32. Letter from James Madison to W. T. Barry (Aug. 4, 1822), *reprinted in* 9 THE WRITINGS OF JAMES MADISON 103 (Gaillard Hunt ed., 1910).

33. ALEXANDER MEIKLEJOHN, POLITICAL FREEDOM: THE CONSTITU-
TIONAL POWERS OF THE PEOPLE 26–27 (1965). Compare John
Dewey: "There can be no public without full publicity in respect
to all consequences which concern it. Whatever obstructs and
restricts publicity, limits and distorts thinking on social affairs."
DEWEY, *supra* note 24, at 167.

34. MEIKLEJOHN, *supra* note 33, at 26.

35. *Id.*

36. There are exceptional cases when a speaker is deemed, in the eyes
of the First Amendment, to be merely "a proxy or fiduciary with
obligations to present those views and voices which are represen-
tative of his community and which would otherwise, by necessity,
be barred from the airwaves." Red Lion Broad. Co. v. FCC, 395
U.S. 367, 389 (1969). In such circumstances the First Amendment
has been interpreted to permit the regulation of speakers' rights
along explicitly Meiklejohnian lines. For a full discussion, *see* Robert Post, *Subsidized Speech*, 106 YALE L. J. 151 (1996).

37. *See, e.g.,* Lamont v. Postmaster General of the U.S., 381 U.S. 301
(1965); Kleindienst v. Mandel, 408 U.S. 753, 762 (1972).

38. Richmond Newspapers, Inc. v. Virginia, 448 U.S. 555, 576–77, 580
(1980). *See* Press-Enterprise Co. v. Superior Court, 478 U.S. 1
(1986); Press-Enterprise Co. v. Superior Court, 464 U.S. 501 (1984);
Globe Newspaper Co. v. Superior Court, 457 U.S. 596 (1982); *see
also* In re New York Times Co., 828 F.2d 110, 114 (2d Cir. 1987)
(extending the First Amendment right of access to "documents
submitted in connection with judicial proceedings that themselves
implicate the right of access"); Westmoreland v. Columbia Broad.
Sys., 752 F.2d 16, 23 (2d Cir. 1984) (holding that the First Amendment presumption of public access attaches to civil as well as
criminal proceedings).

39. Houchins v. KQED, 438 U.S. 1, 12 (1978). Congress took up this
task in the Freedom of Information Act (FOIA). It is something of
a disappointment that even though the Supreme Court has recognized that FOIA was enacted to implement "'a general philosophy
of full agency disclosure,'" Dep't of Air Force v. Rose, 425 U.S.
352, 360 (1976) (quoting S.Rep. No. 813, 89th Cong., 1st Sess., at
3 (1965)), it has nevertheless tended to construe the statute in ways

that have expanded the ability of administrative agencies to with-hold information. *See generally* Martin E. Halstuk & Bill F. Chamberlin, *The Freedom of Information Act 1966–2006: A Retrospective on the Rise of Privacy Protection over the Public Interest in Knowing What the Government's Up To*, 11 COMM. L. & POL'Y 511 (2006).

40. Houchins, 438 U.S. at 14 (Quoting Potter Stewart, *"Or of the Press,"* 26 HASTINGS L.J. 631, 636 (1975)). *See id.* at 16 ("The First and Fourteenth Amendments do not guarantee the public a right of access to information generated or controlled by government.") (Opinion of Stewart, J.); Saxbe v. Washington Post Co., 417 U.S. 843 (1974); Pell v. Procunier, 417 U.S. 817 (1974).

41. *See, e.g.,* STEPHEN HOLMES & CASS R. SUNSTEIN, THE COST OF RIGHTS : WHY LIBERTY DEPENDS ON TAXES (1999).

42. There seems to be general agreement that democratic competence is a constitutional value. Thus the Court has referred to the Freedom of Information Act (FOIA), which enables persons to learn about official government records, as "a structural necessity in a real democracy." Nat'l Archives & Records Admin.v. Favish, 541 U.S. 157, 172 (2004). In one of his first acts as president, Obama reaffirmed his commitment to FOIA because "democracy requires accountability, and accountability requires transparency. . . . In our democracy, the Freedom of Information Act, which encourages accountability through transparency, is the most prominent expression of a profound national commitment to ensuring an open Government." *See* Barack Obama, *Freedom of Information Act*, THE WHITE HOUSE, http://www.whitehouse.gov/the_press_office/FreedomofInformationAct (last visited Apr. 11, 2011). Courts like the European Court of Human Rights have determined that in certain contexts persons have a right to demand information from the government. Társaság a Szabadságjogokért v. Hungary, App, No. 37374/05, Eur. Ct. H.R. (2009), *available at* http://cmiskp .echr.coe.int/tkp197/view.asp?action=html&documentId=849278 &portal=hbkm&source=externalbydocnumber&table=F69A27 FD8FB86142BF01C1166DEA398649. See also Claude Reyes v. Chile, 2006 Inter-Am. Ct. H.R. (ser. C) No. 151 (2006) *available at* http://www.elaw.org/node/2546 ("Democratic control by society,

through public opinion, fosters transparency in State activities and promotes the accountability of State officials in relation to their public activities. Hence, for the individual to be able to exercise democratic control, the State must guarantee access to the information of public interest that it holds. By permitting the exercise of this democratic control, the State encourages greater participation by the individual in the interests of society." *Id.* At ¶ 87); Ontario (Public Safety and Security) v. Criminal Lawyers' Ass'n, [2010] 1 S.C.R. 815, at ¶¶ 30–31 ("the scope of § 2(b) protection includes a right to access to documents only where access is necessary to permit meaningful discussion on a matter of public importance, subject to privileges and functional constraints."). On the debate in the United States concerning the constitutional underpinnings of FOIA, *compare* Thomas I. Emerson, *The First Amendment and the Right to Know: Legal Foundations of the Right to Know,* 1976 WASH. U.L.Q. (1976), and Anthony Lewis, *A Public Right to Know About Public Institutions: The First Amendment as a Sword,* 1980 SUP. CT. REV. 1 (1980), *with* Lillian BeVier, *An Informed Public, an Informing Presss: The Search for a Constitutional Principle,* 68 CAL. L. REV. 482 (1980).

43. Valentine v. Chrestensen, 316 U.S. 52, 54 (1942), *overruled by* Va. State Bd. of Pharmacy v. Va. Citizens Consumer Council, Inc., 425 U.S. 748 (1976).

44. *Va. State Bd. of Pharmacy,* 425 U.S. at 765.

45. Lochner v. New York, 198 U.S. 45, 75 (1905) (Holmes, J., dissenting).

46. Bates v. State Bar of Ariz., 433 U.S. 350, 364 (1977).

47. 44 Liquormart, Inc. v. Rhode Island, 517 U.S. 484, 512 (1996) (plurality opinion). This explanation of the constitutional protections extended to commercial speech is developed in Robert Post, *The Constitutional Status of Commercial Speech,* 48 UCLA L. REV. 1 (2000) (*"Commercial Speech"*). For further thoughts about recent developments in commercial speech doctrine, see Robert Post, *Transparent and Efficient Markets: Compelled Commercial Speech and Coerced Commercial Association in* United Foods, Zauderer, *and* Abood, 40 VAL. U. L. REV. 555 (2006) (*"Compelled Commercial Speech"*).

48. *See, e.g.,* Innovative Database Systems v. Morales, 990 F.2d 217 (5th Cir. 1993); United Reporting Publishing Corp. v. California Highway Patrol, 146 F.3d 1133, 1137 (9th Cir. 1998), *rev'd on other grounds,* 528 U.S. 32 (1999); Individual Reference Services Group, Inc. v. FTC, 145 F.Supp.2d 6, 41 (D.D.C. 2001), *aff'd sub nom.* Trans Union LLC v. F.T.C., 295 F.3d 42, (D.C. Cir. 2002); *cf.* N.Y. State Rest. Ass'n v. New York City Bd. of Health, 556 F.3d 114 (2d Cir. 2009); IMS Health Inc. v. Sorrell, 630 F.3d 263 (2nd Cir. 2010), *cert. granted,* 131 S.Ct. 857 (2011); IMS Health Inc. V. Mills, 616 F.3d 7 (1st Cir. 2010); IMS Health Inc. v. Ayotte, 550 F.3d 42 (1st Cir. 2008); Pharm. Care Mgmt. Ass'n v. Rowe, 429 F.3d 294, 309 (1st Cir. 2005); Robert Post, *Prescribing Records and the First Amendment—New Hampshire's Data-Mining Statute,* 360 NEW ENG. J. MED. 745.

49. Cent. Hudson Gas & Elec. Corp. v. Public Services Commission, 447 U.S. 557, 563 (1980).

50. Zauderer v. Office of Disciplinary Counsel, 471 U.S. 626, 650–51 (1985).

51. First Nat'l Bank v. Bellotti, 435 U.S. 765, 783 (1978) (quoting Va. State Bd. of Pharmacy v. Va. Consumer Council, Inc., 425 U.S. 748, 764 (1976)).

52. "In commercial speech cases, then, a four-part analysis has developed. At the outset, we must determine whether the expression is protected by the First Amendment. For commercial speech to come within that provision, it at least must concern lawful activity and not be misleading. Next, we ask whether the asserted governmental interest is substantial. If both inquiries yield positive answers, we must determine whether the regulation directly advances the governmental interest asserted, and whether it is not more extensive than is necessary to serve that interest." *Cent. Hudson Gas & Elec. Corp.,* 447 U.S. at 566.

53. *See, e.g.,* Oxycal Lab., Inc. v. Jeffers, 909 F.Supp. 719, 723–24 (S.D. Cal. 1995):

> The Government may regulate commercial speech in ways that it may not regulate other speech. Specifically, the government may regulate commercial speech to ensure that it is not

false, deceptive or misleading. Commercial speech that is found to be false or misleading is afforded no First Amendment Protection at all. This is because a listener "has little interest in receiving false, misleading, or deceptive commercial information." However, if speech is found to be noncommercial speech, even falsehoods contained in the speech will be given protection. The Supreme Court has made clear that Constitutional protection does not turn upon "the truth . . . of the ideas and beliefs which are offered." . . .

> The erroneous statement is inevitable in free debate, and . . . it must be protected if the freedoms of expression are to have the "breathing space" that they "need . . . to survive."

New York Times Co. v. Sullivan, 376 U.S. 254, 271–72 (1964) (citations omitted). Therefore, if false or misleading speech is non-commercial it is afforded full First Amendment protection, and if it is commercial, it falls entirely outside the protection of the First Amendment, and would be subject to prior restraints. . . .

54. Edenfield v. Fane, 507 U.S. 761, 768 (1993) (quoting Va. State Bd. of Pharmacy v. Va. Citizens Consumer Council, Inc., 425 U.S. 748, 771–72 (1976)).

55. There is "a vast regulatory apparatus in both the federal government and the states . . . to control . . . potentially misleading or deceptive speech." Kathleen M. Sullivan, *Cheap Spirits, Cigarettes, and Free Speech: The Implications of* 44 Liquormart, 1996 SUP. CT. REV. 123, 153.

56. Milavetz, Gallop & Milavetz, P.A. v. United States, 130 S.Ct. 1324, 1339–1341 (2010); Post, *Compelled Commercial Speech, supra* note 47, at 584–85. In the context of public discourse, the Court has specifically held that compelled disclosure of facts should be subject to strict scrutiny. *See* Riley v. Nat'l Fed'n of the Blind, 487 U.S. 781 (1988).

57. Miami Herald Pub. Co. v. Tornillo, 418 U.S. 241 (1974).

58. Thus the Court has held that that state cannot even force participants in public discourse to disclose their identity; it has affirmed

a constitutional right to publish anonymously. *See* McIntyre v. Ohio Elections Comm'n., 514 U.S. 334 (1995).

59. In *United States v. United Foods, Inc.,* 533 U.S. 405 (2001), the Court held that the State was constitutionally prohibited from compelling commercial speakers to communicate messages of opinion and endorsement, as distinct from neutral factual information. Because the commercial context of these messages was outside public discourse, *United Foods* necessarily rests on the recognition of an autonomy interest in speakers that does not derive from democratic legitimation. The recognition of such an interest is most unusual in the Court's jurisprudence, and it was not well thought through. *See* Post, *Compelled Commercial Speech, supra* note 47. The Court has been confused and inconsistent in determining the kind of legal protection that this kind of autonomy interest should receive. *See* United States v. United Foods, Inc., 533 U.S. 405, 410 (2001); Glickman v. Wileman Bros. & Elliott, 521 U.S. 457, 491–92 (1997) (Souter, J., dissenting); Johanns v. Livestock Mktg. Ass'n, 544 U.S. 550, 566 n.10 (2005) (Souter, J., dissenting); Post, *Compelled Commercial Speech, supra* note 47.

60. *See, e.g.,* Birmingham v. Fodor's Travel Publ'ns, Inc., 833 P.2d 70, 78–79 (Hawaii 1992).

61. ANTHONY GIDDENS, BEYOND LEFT AND RIGHT: THE FUTURE OF RADICAL POLITICS 128 (1994).

62. Doctors, for example, commit malpractice for failing to inform patients in a timely way of an accurate diagnosis, for failing to give patients proper instructions, for failing to ask patients necessary questions, or for failing to refer a patient to an appropriate specialist. *See* Smith v. Walker, 708 So.2d 797 (La. Ct. of App. 1998); Malone v. Louisiana, 569 So.2d 1098 (La. Ct. of App. 1990); Axelrad v. Jackson, 142 S.W.3d 418 (Tex. Ct. of App. 2004); Morgan v. Engles, 127 N.W.2d 382, 383 (Mich. 1964). *See generally* Canterbury v. Spence, 464 F.2d 772, 781 (D.C. Cir. 1972) (citations omitted):

> The cases demonstrate that the physician is under an obligation to communicate specific information to the patient when the exigencies of reasonable care call for it. Due care may require a physician perceiving symptoms of bodily abnormality

to alert the patient to the condition. It may call upon the physician confronting an ailment which does not respond to his ministrations to inform the patient thereof. It may command the physician to instruct the patient as to any limitations to be presently observed for his own welfare, and as to any precautionary therapy he should seek in the future. It may oblige the physician to advise the patient of the need for or desirability of any alternative treatment promising greater benefit than that being pursued. Just as plainly, due care normally demands that the physician warn the patient of any risks to his well-being which contemplated therapy may involve.

63. *See, e.g.*, CONSUMERS FOR DENTAL CHOICE, WORKING TO ABOLISH MERCURY DENTAL FILLINGS, http://www.toxicteeth.org/about_Us .cfm; MERCURY POLICY PROJECT, http://www.mercurypolicy.org.

64. *See, e.g.*, Edenfield v. Fane, 507 U.S. 761, 774–75 (1993); Shapero v. Ky. Bar Ass'n, 486 U.S. 466, 474 (1988); Zauderer v. Office of Disciplinary Counsel, 471 U.S. 626, 642 (1985); Ohralik v. Ohio State Bar Ass'n, 436 U.S. 447, 465 (1978).

65. As is the case in a recent South Dakota statute that seeks to discourage abortions by requiring doctors falsely to inform their patients about the likelihood of post abortion syndrome. The statute is discussed in detail in Robert Post, *Informed Consent to Abortion: A First Amendment Analysis of Compelled Physician Speech*, 2007 ILL. L. REV. 939.

66. See, for example, *Conant v. Walters*, in which the Ninth Circuit reached just this conclusion in the context of the federal government seeking to prevent doctors from "recommending" (as distinct from "prescribing") medical marijuana. 309 F.3d 629 (9th Cir. 2002). The court believed that First Amendment scrutiny was triggered because "An integral component of the practice of medicine is the communication between a doctor and a patient. Physicians must be able to speak frankly and openly to patients." *Id.* at 636. Even though federal law prohibited the prescription and use of marijuana, a patient might "upon receiving the recommendation . . . petition the government to change the law." *Id.* at 634.

67. Planned Parenthood v. Heineman, 724 F.Supp.2nd 1025, 1048 (D. Neb.2010). The Court granted a preliminary injunction enjoining enforcement of the Nebraska statute. A similar statute has recently been enacted by South Dakota. See http://legis.state.sd.us/sessions/2011/Bill.aspx?File=HB1217HJU.htm.

68. 11 U.S.C. § 526(a)(4). See Samuel L. Bufford & Erwin Chemerinsky, *Constitutional Problems in the 2005 Bankruptcy Amendments*, 82 AM. BANKR. L.J. 1 (2008); Erwin Chemerinsky, *Constitutional Issues Posed in the Bankruptcy Abuse Prevention and Consumer Protection Act of 2005*, 79 AM. BANKR. L.J. 571 (2005); Robin Huffman, *Bankruptcy and Free Speech: New Bankruptcy Code Provisions Restrict Attorneys' Right to Properly Advise Clients*, 35 HASTINGS CONST. L.Q. 118 (2006); Robert Wann, Jr., *"Debt Relief Agencies": Does the Bankruptcy Abuse Prevention and Consumer Protection Act of 2005 Violate Attorneys' First Amendment Rights?*, 14 AM. BANKR. INST. L. REV. 273 (2006).

69. In re Reyes, 361 B.R. 276 (S.D. Fla. 2007), *aff'd in part, rev'd in part*, No. 07-20689-CIV, 2007 WL 6082567 (S.D. Fla. Dec. 19, 2007); Milavetz, Gallop & Milavetz, A.P. v. United States, 355 B.R. 758, 768 (D. Minn. 2006), *rev'd*, 541 F.3d 785 (8th Cir. 2008), *aff'd in part, rev'd in part*, 130 S.Ct. 1324 (2010); In re Attorneys at Law & Debt Relief Agencies, 332 B.R. 66 (S.D. Ga. 2005).

70. *See* Hersch v. United States, 553 F.3d 743 (5th Cir. 2008), *cert. denied*, 130 S.Ct. 1878 (2010); *Milavetz*, 541 F.3d 785, *aff'd in part, rev'd in part*, 130 S.Ct. 1324 (2010); Conn. Bar Ass'n v. United States, 394 B.R. 274 (D. Conn. 2008), *aff'd in part, vacated in part*, 620 F.3d 81 (2d Cir. 2010); Zelotes v. Adams, 363 B.R. 660 (D. Conn. 2007), *rev'd*, 606 F.3d 34 (2d Cir. 2010); Olsen v. Gonzales, 350 B.R. 906 (D. Or. 2006), *aff'd on reh'g*, 368 B.R. 886 (D. Or. 2007), *aff'd in part, rev'd in part sub nom. Olsen v. Holder*, 402 F. App'x 311 (9th Cir. 2010).

71. *Milavetz*, 355 B.R. at 765; 541 F.3d at 793–94. "Moreover, it may be in the client's best interest to incur additional debt to purchase a reliable automobile before filing for bankruptcy, so that the debtor will have dependable transportation to travel to and from work, which will likely be necessary to maintain the debtor's payments in bankruptcy. Incurring these types of additional secured debt,

which would often survive or could be reaffirmed by the debtor, may be in the debtor's best interest without harming the creditors." *Id.* at 794.

72. *Olsen,* 350 B.R. at 916.

73. *Zelotes,* 363 B.R. at 665–66.

74. *Milavetz,* 541 F.3d at 793; *Olsen,* 350 B.R. at 916; *Zelotes,* 363 B.R. at 665–67; *Conn. Bar Ass'n,* 394 B.R. at 284. The only possible exception might be *Hersh,* 553 F.3d 743 (5th Cir. 2008), which agreed that "if interpreted literally" BAPCPA "may apply to speech that is protected by the First Amendment." *Id.* at 754. The Fifth Circuit chose to apply "the doctrine of constitutional avoidance" to construe "the statute to prevent only a debt relief agency's advice to a debtor to incur debt in contemplation of bankruptcy when doing so would be an abuse of the bankruptcy system," *id.* at 756–57, which the court interpreted as prohibiting attorney advice to commit "a fraudulent act." *Id; see id.* at 758–60. The Court explicitly held that as so interpreted BAPCPA "has no application to good faith advice to engage in conduct that is consistent with a debtor's interest and does not abuse or improperly manipulate the bankruptcy system." *Id.* at 761.

75. Milavetz, Gallop & Milavetz, A.P. v. United States, 130 S.Ct. 1324, 1335–36 (2010).

76. *Id.* at 1336. The Court explained:

> That "[n]o other solution yields as sensible a" result further persuades us of the correctness of this narrow reading. . . . It would make scant sense to prevent attorneys and other debt relief agencies from advising individuals thinking of filing for bankruptcy about options that would be beneficial to both those individuals and their creditors. That construction serves none of the purposes of the Bankruptcy Code or the amendments enacted through the BAPCPA. . . . For the same reason, we reject Milavetz's suggestion that § 526(a)(4) broadly prohibits debt relief agencies from discussing covered subjects instead of merely proscribing affirmative advice to undertake a particular action.

Id. at 1337.

77. *Id.* The Court pointedly gestured to ABA Model Rule of Professional Conduct 1.2(d) (2009): "A lawyer shall not counsel a client to engage, or assist a client, in conduct that the lawyer knows is criminal or fraudulent, but a lawyer may discuss the legal consequences of any proposed course of conduct with client and may counsel or assist a client to make a good faith effort to determine the validity, scope, meaning or application of the law." *Id.* at 1337–38. The Court chose not to reach the question of whether the statute, construed in this narrow fashion, "withstands First Amendment scrutiny." *Id.* at 1339.

78. *See* text at note 75 *supra.*

79. *See* note 77 *supra.*

80. *See* Jespersen v. Zubiate-Beauchamp, 7 Cal. Rptr. 3d 715, 720–21 (Ct. App. 2003):

> [A]ppellants' conduct allegedly consisted of: (1) a failure to serve timely discovery responses . . . ; (2) a failure to comply with a court order to serve responses without objections; and (3) a failure to comply with a second court order. Thus, it appears that the alleged attorney malpractice did not consist of any act in furtherance of anyone's right of petition or free speech, but appellants' negligent failure to do so on behalf of their clients. . . . Appellants have failed to demonstrate that such conduct amounts to constitutionally protected speech or petition, and we reject their attempt to turn garden-variety attorney malpractice into a constitutional right.

Id.

81. Michael R. Siebecker, *Corporate Speech, Securities Regulation, and an Institutional Approach to the First Amendment,* 48 Wm. & Mary L. Rev. 613 (2006); Paul Horwitz, *Universities as First Amendment Institutions: Some Easy Answers and Hard Questions,* 54 UCLA L. Rev. 1497 (2007). An inspiration for this approach has been Frederick Schauer, *Towards an Institutional First Amendment,* 89 Minn. L. Rev. 1256 (2005).

82. Daniel Halberstam, *Commercial Speech, Professional Speech, and the Constitutional Status of Social Institutions,* 147 U. Pa. L. Rev. 771, 777 (1999). *See* Schauer, *supra* note 81, at 1274 (arguing that

the First Amendment ought to "more consciously treat . . . institutions in rulelike fashion" by moving "the inquiry away from direct application of the underlying values of the First Amendment to the conduct at issue and towards the mediating determination of whether the conduct at issue was or was not the conduct of one of these institutions.").

83. There in fact may be no generic constitutional account of what others have called "professional speech," which is to say "speech . . . uttered in the course of professional practice," as distinct from "speech . . . uttered by a professional." Halberstam, *supra* note 82, at 843. The regulation of professional speech will trigger First Amendment coverage to the extent that the regulation threatens to compromise First Amendment values. Sometimes, as in malpractice actions, state regulation of professional speech will not trigger First Amendment coverage at all, and sometimes, as in the case of BAPCPA, such coverage will be triggered by the value of democratic competence. In other cases constitutional review may be provoked by constitutional values different from democratic competence. If a state were to bar clergy from informing parishioners that transubstantiation occurs during holy communion, for example, we would regard the threat to the free formation of religious belief to be of such great significance as to trigger constitutional review under the Free Exercise and Establishment Clauses. This is true even though we would consider the question of transubstantiation to involve matters of opinion rather than of knowledge. And sometimes constitutional coverage might be triggered because state regulation adversely affects institutions that have their own constitutional value. For example, in *Legal Services Corp. v. Velazquez*, 531 U.S. 533 (2001), the Court struck down federal legislation that effectively prevented legal services attorneys from arguing to courts that "either a state or federal statute by its terms or in its application is violative of the United States Constitution." *Id.* at 537. The Court held that the legislation "prohibits speech and expression upon which courts must depend for the proper exercise of the judicial power" and hence "threatens severe impairment of the judicial function." *Id.* at 545–46. The shape and form of con-

stitutional protections extended to professional speech will depend upon the precise constitutional values at stake.

84. *See* Hughes v. Malone, 247 S.E.2d 107, 111 (Ga. Ct. App. 1978) (holding that "[a]lthough an attorney is not an insurer of the results sought to be obtained by such representation, when, after undertaking to accomplish a specific result, he then wilfully or negligently fails to apply commonly known and accepted legal principles and procedures through ignorance of basic, well-established and unambiguous principles of law or through a failure to act reasonably to protect his client's interests, then he has breached his duty toward the client"); *see also* Dixon Ticonderoga Co. v. Estate of O'Connor, 248 F.3d 151, 172 (3d Cir. 2001) (finding a "duty [on the part of an attorney] to take any steps necessary for the proper handling of the matter, to communicate about the matter with [the client], and to advise [the client] about the legal and strategic issues involved in the representation"). The Third Circuit also found a "specific duty to research, monitor, and advise his or her clients about [key legal issues]." *Id.* Indeed, attorneys are required to make a good faith effort to research unfamiliar legal issues, so as to provide their clients with accurate legal advice. *See* Clary v. Lite Machines Corp., 850 N.E.2d 423, 423 (Ind. Ct. App. 2006) (noting that "all of the states . . . that have addressed the issue of legal research (or lack thereof) as malpractice have found that an attorney's duty to his client encompasses knowledge of the law and an obligation to perform diligent research and provide informed judgments"); Prudential Ins. Co. v. Dewey, Ballantine, Bushby, Palmer & Wood, 80 N.Y.2d 377 (N.Y. 1992) (finding attorneys liable for a false opinion letter).

85. *See, e.g.,* Bailey v. Tucker, 621 A.2d 108, 115 (Pa. 1993) (finding that "an attorney who agrees for a fee to represent a client is by implication agreeing to provide that client with professional services consistent with those expected of the profession at large"); Gorski v. Smith, 812 A.2d 683, 700 (Pa. Super. Ct. 2002) (noting that "[t]he rule is well established that an attorney is liable to his client for negligence in rendering professional services . . . [and] that liability will be imposed for want of such skill, prudence and diligence

as lawyers of ordinary skill and capacity commonly possess and exercise"); Young v. Bridwell, 437 P.2d 686, 690 (Utah 1968) (holding that an attorney is "required to possess the ordinary legal knowledge and skill common to members of his profession . . . [or] the ordinary standards of professional competence").

86. *See* note 52 *supra*.

87. Whether commercial speech is misleading is itself a First Amendment question, whereas whether professional speech constitutes malpractice is not a First Amendment question. This is an important difference that is not theorized in contemporary doctrine. One explanation might be that courts feel confident in determining the truth or falsity of commercial information, but they feel rather less confident in determining the trustworthiness of professional advice and judgment. They are therefore inclined to constitutionalize the latter question only in the most extreme situations, such as those created by statutes like BAPCPA.

88. Iowa Board of Dental Examiners, In the Matter of Larry J. Hanus, Findings of Fact, Conclusions of Law, Decision and Order, September 1, 1994, quoted in Office of the Attorney General of the State of Iowa, Opinion No. 02-12-1, December 10, 2002, 2002 WL 31952794 (Iowa A.G.), at *4; Breiner v. Connecticut, No. CV 98061275, 1998 WL 738066 (Conn. Super. Oct. 7, 1998); Bd. of Dental Examiners v. Hufford, 461 N.W. 2d 194 (Iowa 1990).

89. *See, e.g.,* Williams v. Jenkins, 83 S.E.2d 614, 615 (Ga. 1954) (upholding a conviction under "a city ordinance which, in substance, provides that it shall be unlawful to practice within the city the calling or profession of fortune-teller or astrologer.").

90. See, for example, *In re Bartha*, 134 Cal. Rptr. 39 (Ct. App. 1976), in which a court upheld a Los Angeles ordinance providing:

> No person shall advertise by sign, circular, handbill or in any newspaper, periodical or magazine, or other publication or publications, or by any other means, to tell fortunes, to find or restore lost or stolen property, to locate oil wells, gold or silver or other ore or metal or natural product; to restore lost love or friendship or affection, to unite or procure lovers, husbands, wives, lost relatives or friends, for or without pay,

by means of occult or psychic powers, faculties or forces, clairvoyance, psychology, psychometry, spirits, mediumship, seership, prophecy, astrology, palmistry, necromancy, or other craft, science, cards, talismans, charms, potions, magnetism or magnetized articles or substances, oriental mysteries or magic of any kind or nature, or numerology, or to engage in or carry on any business the advertisement of which is prohibited by this section.

Id. at 40. The defendant in the case argued that the statute violated rights to freedom of expression, because it would "prohibit legitimate businesses, such as weather forecasting." *Id.* at 43. The Court rejected the argument on the ground that "[i]t is within the police power of the municipality and province of the legislative body to determine that the business of fortunetelling is inherently deceptive and that its regulation or prohibition is required in order to protect the gullible, superstitious, and unwary." *Id.*

In *David v. Ohio*, 160 N.E. 473 (Ohio 1928), the Ohio Supreme Court upheld a statute providing that "whoever, not having been legally licensed so to do, represents himself to be an astrologer, fortune-teller, clairvoyant or palmister, shall be fined not less than twenty-five dollars nor more than one hundred dollars or imprisoned in jail not less than thirty days nor more than three months, or both." *Id.* at 474. The Court offered a history of legislative efforts to regulate fortune-telling and astrology on the grounds "that fortune-telling and similar crafts are fraudulent practices, and therefore not within the protection afforded to a lawful business." *Id.* at 475.

Compare to these cases the decision of the federal district court in *Rushman v. Milwaukee*, 959 F.Supp. 1040 (E.D. Wisc. 1997), in which, at the behest of an astrologer, the court invoked the First Amendment to strike down a Milwaukee ordinance outlawing "astrology, fortune telling, and numerous other pseudosciences." *Id.* at 1041. The court stated:

The line between beliefs (or opinions) and facts is blurry at best. What seems like a provable fact to one person is only an opinion to another; paleontologists like Stephen J. Gould think that evolution is a scientific fact, while creationists think it is only a false belief. Throughout history, many societies have decided that the government should arbitrate truth and falsehood, fact and opinion; their record is not comforting. Doubting the government's talent for or benefit from declaring what is true and what is not, the United States took a different approach; the First Amendment forbids the government from arbitrating truth and fiction. A person is free to write and sell books declaring the earth is flat or that one race is superior to another.

Although the First Amendment prohibits arbitrating fact and opinion, it allows the government to regulate economic transactions. Therefore, the government can outlaw fraud—false statements made to convince a person to buy an item or invest money. . . .

Although astrology and fortune telling may be rejected by science, naive and outdated, they are beliefs; the marketplace of ideas—not the United States, not Wisconsin, and not the City of Milwaukee—decides their value. Banning those practices is not commercial regulation but censorship. If the City is attacking those who use pseudo-sciences to defraud others, the ordinance is overly broad. The City must focus on the fraud, not the subject-matter of the speech.

Id. at 1041–42. As the court's reference to the publication of flat-earth books makes clear, the district court understood the ordinance to prohibit the practice of astrology in public discourse, rather than merely to prohibit fraud between commercial actors. The Court's opinion illustrates how First Amendment doctrine ensures that public discourse remain a realm of opinion rather than knowledge.

91. Illinois *ex rel.* Madigan v. Telemarketing Assoc., Inc., 538 U.S. 600, 612 (2003) ("The First Amendment does not shield fraud.").

92. Consider *Turner v. Kansas City*, 191 S.W.2d 612 (Mo. 1946), in which the Court upheld the constitutionality of a city ordinance that provided:

> It shall be unlawful for any person for pay to tell or pretend
> to tell fortunes or reveal or attempt to reveal future events in
> the life of another or by means of occult or psychic powers,
> faculties or forces, clairvoyance, psychology, psychometry,
> spirit-mediumship, prophecy, astrology, palmistry, necro-
> mance, cards, talismans, charms, potions, magnetism or mag-
> netized articles or substances, oriental mysteries or magic of
> any kind or nature, to undertake or pretend to find or restore
> lost or stolen money or property, to undertake or pretend to
> locate oil wells, gold or silver or other ore or metal or natural
> product, to undertake or pretend to restore lost love, friend-
> ship or affection, to undertake or pretend to unite, or reunite
> or to find lovers, husbands, wives, lost relatives or friends.

Id. at 613. The plaintiff in the case conducted "a business 'commonly known as fortune telling' for pay," *id.*, and sued to invali-
date the ordinance. She argued that prohibiting "any person to
'reveal or attempt to reveal future events in the life of another'"
was "unreasonable" because it would "prevent engineers advising
contractors how to achieve given construction results; a physician
advising a patient how to improve his health; a lawyer applying the
law to facts related by his client; a scientist advising a manufac-
turer how to produce a synthetic product; a banker advising a cus-
tomer he will extend credit; an inventor predicting he will enable
people to overcome space at unheard of heights and speeds, and a
radio genius predicting he will carry the human voice from city to
city, state to state, and nation to nation." *Id.* at 617. The Court
would have none of it:

> Plaintiff is not engaged in any of the endeavors last above
> specified. Usually a litigant champions his own rights; not
> the rights of others. The ordinance, read as a whole, evi-
> dences a purpose to protect against deception and fraud
> through the suppression of the acts therein enumerated. In so
> far as the matters mentioned by plaintiff are the result of le-
> gitimate business endeavors, they are without the pale of the
> ordinance provisions. Plaintiff's position twists the language

and warps the manifest purpose of the ordinance. It is without merit. . . . It will be soon enough to rule individual instances under the ordinance as they occur and are presented.

Id. at 617–18.

93. *See, e.g.,* New Jersey v. Kennilworth, 54 A. 244 (N.J. 1903) (upholding a 1799 statute providing that "all persons who shall use or pretend to use or have skill in physiognomy, palmistry or like crafty science, * * * shall be deemed and adjudged to be disorderly persons," with the proviso that "[i]f ever there shall be discovered any rational evidence that palmistry is a real science, its use for honest purposes will pass beyond the range of this statute; but, in the present case, the use of palmistry was plainly within the prohibition."); Griffith v. Dep't of Motor Vehicles, 598 P.2d 1377, 1382–83 (Wash. Ct. App. 1979) (upholding a ban on "drugless healers" performing "natural childbirths" by comparing the adequate training obtained by obstetricians to the inadequate training obtained by "drugless healers" and declaring the ban a "legitimate regulatory expression where the legislature seeks to prevent the inadequately trained and uneducated from practicing in areas in which competency is lacking").

94. Homeopathic medicine remains controversial within the mainstream medical community. In reviewing the literature on the overall effectiveness of homeopathic medicine, the American Medical Association (AMA) concluded, "While most homeopathic remedies are not known to have harmed anyone (probably because of the extreme dilutions involved), the efficacy of most homeopathic remedies has not been proven." AMERICAN MEDICAL ASSOCIATION, REPORT 12 OF THE COUNCIL ON SCIENTIFIC AFFAIRS 9 (1998), *available at* http://www.idt.mdh.se/kurser/ct3340/ht07/assignment-2-extra-articles/Alternative%20Medicine.pdf.

95. Consider in this regard *In re Guess*, 393 S.E.2d 833 (N.C. 1990), in which the Supreme Court of North Carolina upheld the revocation of a doctor's license to practice medicine for "unprofessional conduct" because he had practiced homeopathic medicine. The court held that whether "new and beneficial medical practices" would be permitted must be determined "by 'acceptable and pre-

vailing' methods of medical research, experimentation, testing, and approval." *Id.* at 839. By contrast, the dissent proclaimed that "this is not a case of a quack beguiling the public with snake oil and drums, but a dedicated physician seeking to find new ways to relieve human suffering." *Id.* at 841 (Frye, J., dissenting).

96. For a brief history of the debate about government control of the accounting profession, see Ronald M. Mano & Jeff A. Barton, *Under the Federal Microscope,* 40 NAT'L PUB. ACCT. 15 (1995).

97. *See, e.g.,* V. E. Odmark, *Some Aspects of the Evolution of Accounting Functions,* 29 THE ACCOUNTING REVIEW 634, 634–38 (1954) ("As the interpretor of business results, the accountant must utilize all methods and techniques available to him in discharging his obligations to management and to society. A corporate investor must be furnished with information which will permit him to form an opinion as to the profitableness of operations of the enterprise. 'Fool's' profits resulting from monetary inflation as well as losses from monetary deflation must be clearly indicated.").

98. R. K. MAUTZ & HUSSEIN A. SHARAF, THE PHILOSOPHY OF AUDITING 14 (1961) ("Accounting includes the collection, classification, summarization, and communication of financial data; it involves the measurement and communication of business events and conditions as they affect and represent a given enterprise or other entity. The task of accounting is to reduce a tremendous mass of detailed information to manageable and understandable portions.").

3
Academic Freedom and the
Production of Disciplinary Knowledge

1. Keyishian v. Bd. of Regents, 385 U.S. 589, 603 (1967).

2. J. Peter Byrne, *Academic Freedom: A "Special Concern of the First Amendment,"* 99 YALE. L.J. 251, 253 (1989).

3. *Keyishian,* 385 U.S. at 603. *See* Rosenberger v. Rectors and Visitors of the Univ. of Va., 515 U.S. 819, 831 (1995); Healy v. James, 408 U.S. 169, 180 (1972); Dambrot v. Cent. Mich. Univ., 55 F.3d 1177, 1188 (6th Cir. 1995) ("The purpose of the free-speech clause . . .

is to protect the market in ideas, broadly understood as the public expression of ideas, narratives, concepts, imagery, opinions—scientific, political, or aesthetic—to an audience whom the speaker seeks to inform, edify, or entertain."); Thomas Gibbs Gee, *'Enemies or Allies?' In Defense of Judges*, 66 Tex. L. Rev. 1617, 1617 (1988) (referring to "academic freedom and to the all but indistinguishable first amendment right of free speech").

4. Karl Jaspers, The Idea of the University 2 (H. A. T. Reiche and H. F. Vanderschmidt trans., 1959).

5. *What Is Harvard's Mission Statement?*, Harvard University, http://www.harvard.edu/siteguide/faqs/faq110.html (last visited March 8, 2008). For a good survey, see R. George Wright, *The Emergence of First Amendment Academic Freedom*, 85 Neb. L. Rev. 793 (2007).

6. David Madsen, *Review Essay: The American University in a Changing Society: Three Views*, 91 Am. J. Educ. 356, 361 (1983). *See* Harry D. Gideonse, *Changing Issues of Academic Freedom*, 94 Proc. Am. Phil. Soc. 91, 92 (1950) ("The function of a university is the discovery and the dissemination of the truth in all branches of learning.").

7. D. C. Gilman, The Benefits Which Society Derives from Universities: An Address 16 (1885). Gilman's view should be contrasted with John Henry Newman's assertion in 1852 that the *"essence"* of a university is the *"teaching* of universal *knowledge,"* which for Newman implied that the purpose of a university was "the diffusion and extension of knowledge rather than the advancement. If its object were scientific and philosophical discovery, I do not see why a University should have students." John Henry Newman, The Idea of a University 3 (Frank M. Turner ed., 1996).

8. Arthur Twining Hadley, the president of Yale, noted in 1903 that "[i]n Germany the increase of academic freedom is to a surprisingly large measure the result of public interest in modern science and public demand for competent and trained technical experts." Arthur Twining Hadley, *Academic Freedom in Theory and Practice*, 91 Atlantic Monthly 334, 341 (1903).

9. John Dewey, *Academic Freedom*, 23 Educ. Rev. 1, 1 (1902). "The

university function is the truth-function. At one time it may be more concerned with the tradition or transmission of truth, and at another time with its discovery. Both functions are necessary, and neither can ever be entirely absent." *Id.* at 3. For an example of how academic freedom would appear under the more traditional concept of education, *see* Kay v. Bd. of Higher Educ. of New York, 18 N.Y.S. 2d 821, 829 (N.Y. Sup. Ct 1940) (upholding the dismissal of Bertrand Russell from the College of the City of New York on the grounds that "this court . . . will not tolerate academic freedom being used as a cloak to promote the popularization in the minds of adolescents of acts forbidden by the penal Law. . . . Academic freedom does not mean academic license. It is the freedom to do good and not to teach evil. . . . Academic freedom cannot teach that . . . adultery is attractive and good for the community. There are norms and criteria of truth which have been recognized by the founding fathers.").

10. This is not the only justification for academic freedom, for universities have other purposes besides the advancement of knowledge. They also have the pedagogical purpose of inculcating in their students a mature independence of mind. Important aspects of academic freedom are necessary to serve this distinct purpose. *See* Robert Post, *The Structure of Academic Freedom, in* ACADEMIC FREEDOM AFTER SEPTEMBER 11 (Zone Press, Beshara Doumani, ed., 2006).

11. Arthur O. Lovejoy, *Academic Freedom, in* ENCYCLOPEDIA OF THE SOCIAL SCIENCES 384–85 (Edwin R. A. Seligman & Alvin Johnson eds., 1930).

12. The Declaration is reprinted in AMERICAN ASSOCIATION OF UNIVERSITY PROFESSORS, POLICY DOCUMENTS AND REPORTS 291–301 (9th ed. 2001) ("AAUP DOCUMENTS"). Its major authors included Edwin R. A. Seligman and Arthur O. Lovejoy. *See* Walter P. Metzger, *The 1940 Statement of Principles on Academic Freedom and Tenure,* 53 LAW & CONTEMP. PROBS. 3, 12–13 (1990).

13. AAUP DOCUMENTS, *supra* note 12, at 3–11.

14. William W. Van Alstyne, *Academic Freedom and the First Amendment in the Supreme Court of the United States: An Unhurried Historical Review,* 53 LAW & CONTEMP. PROBS. 79, 79 (1990). *See*

Browzin v. Catholic Univ. of Am., 527 F.2d 843, 848 & n. 8 (D.C. Cir. 1975) ("[The 1940 Statement] represent[s] widely shared norms within the academic community, having achieved acceptance by organizations which represent teachers as well as organizations which represent college administrators and governing boards.").

15. *1915 Declaration, supra* note 12, at 292.

16. *1940 Statement, supra* note 13, at 3–4:

> Academic Freedom
>
> 1. Teachers are entitled to full freedom in research and in the publication of the results, subject to the adequate performance of their other academic duties; but research for pecuniary return should be based upon an understanding with the authorities of the institution.
>
> 2. Teachers are entitled to freedom in the classroom in discussing their subject, but they should be careful not to introduce into their teaching controversial matter which has no relation to their subject. Limitations of academic freedom because of religious or other aims of the institution should be clearly stated in writing at the time of the appointment.
>
> 3. College and university teachers are citizens, members of a learned profession, and officers of an educational institution. When they speak or write as citizens, they should be free from institutional censorship or discipline, but their special position in the community imposes special obligations. As scholars and educational officers, they should remember that the public may judge their profession and their institution by their utterances. Hence they should at all times be accurate, should exercise appropriate restraint, should show respect for the opinions of others, and should make every effort to indicate that they are not speaking for the institution.

17. *Id.*

18. *Declaration, supra* note 12, at 295.

19. *Id.*
20. *Id.* at 294.
21. *Id.* at 300.
22. *Id.* at 298. On the relationship between academic freedom and a theory of knowledge, see John R. Searle, *Two Concepts of Academic Freedom, in* 88–89 THE CONCEPT OF ACADEMIC FREEDOM 92 (Edmund L. Pincoffs ed., 1975).
23. *Declaration, supra* note 12, at 298.
24. For a discussion, see MATTHEW W. FINKIN & ROBERT C. POST, FOR THE COMMON GOOD: PRINCIPLES OF AMERICAN ACADEMIC FREEDOM (2009).
25. David M. Rabban, *Does Academic Freedom Limit Faculty Autonomy?,* 66 TEX. L. REV. 1405, 1408–9 (1988). Lovejoy accurately caught the tension between individual freedom and professional obligations when he defined academic freedom as

> the freedom of the teacher or research worker in higher institutions of learning to investigate and discuss the problems of his science and to express his conclusions, whether through publication or in the instruction of students, without interference from political or ecclesiastical authority, or from the administrative officials of the institution in which he is employed, unless his methods are found by qualified bodies of his own profession to be clearly incompetent or contrary to professional ethics.

Lovejoy, *supra* note 11, at 384; *see also* Philip Selznick, *"Law in Context" Revisited,* 30 J. L. & SOC. 177, 181 (2003):

> Consider, for example, the ideal of academic freedom. The rights and duties of teachers and students are neither absolute nor self-justifying. They derive from our understanding of what teaching, learning, and scholarship require. . . . [The rights of academic freedom] are framed and limited by norms of scholarly achievement, professional ethics, and academic government.

26. "Academic freedom is not a doctrine to insulate a teacher from evaluation by the institution that employs him." Carley v. Ariz. Bd. of Regents, 737 P.2d 1099, 1103 (Ariz. App. 1987).

27. Robert M. Hutchins, *The Meaning and Significance of Academic Freedom*, 300 ANNALS AM. ACAD. POL. & SOC. SCI. 72, 72–73 (July 1955).

28. Nicholas Murray Butler, the President of Columbia University who notoriously fired Columbia professors who opposed American entry into World War I, see Post, *supra* note 10, demonstrated his ignorance of the essence of academic freedom when he asserted that "a university teacher owes a decent respect to the opinions of mankind. Men who feel that their personal convictions require them to treat the mature opinion of the civilized world without respect or with active contempt may well be given an opportunity to do so from private station and without the added influence and prestige of a university's name." Nicholas Murray Butler, *Academic Freedom*, 47 EDUC. REV. 291, 292 (1914). For Butler, "the crux of the whole matter" was that those who enjoyed "academic freedom" were required to do so "as gentlemen." *Id.* at 294. In *Science* the philosopher J. E. Creighton cut to the heart of the matter by quoting at length from an 1897 address of Cornell President Schurman: "'If it is asserted that the business of the college or university is to teach that which the average man may believe, or that which is acceptable to the university, or that which the board of trustees may assert as truth, the answer must always be that such a course contravenes the principle on which the university was founded, and however true it may be that the majority must rule in the body politic, the motto of the university must be, one man with God's truth is a majority.'" Quoted in J. E. Creighton, *Academic Freedom* 37 SCI.450, 450 (1921). Schurman went on to argue that this is because "'the end of a university is truth and the promotion of truth. . . . We need for the advance of civilization the striking out of new ideas or the application of old ideas to new fields. Where are such ideas to be urged, if the business of the university is to teach what is acceptable to the community? All science would be impossible on this theory.'" *Id.*

29. Hutchins, *supra* note 27, at 73. Kant saw this very clearly:

> It is absolutely essential that the learned community at the university also contain a faculty that is independent of the government's command with regard to its teachings; one that . . .

is free to evaluate everything, and concerns itself with the interests of the sciences, that is, with truth: one in which reason is authorized to speak out publicly. For without a faculty of this kind, the truth would not come to light (and this would be to the government's own detriment); but reason is by its nature free and admits of no command to hold something as true (no imperative "Believe" but only a free "I believe").

IMMANUEL KANT, THE CONFLICT OF THE FACULTIES 27–29 (J. Gregor trans., 1979).

30. Charles W. Eliot, *Academic Freedom*, 26 SCI. 1, 1 (July 5, 1907).

31. Hence the observation of the *1915 Declaration:*

> This brings us to the most serious difficulty of the problem; namely, the dangers connected with the existence in a democracy of an overwhelming and concentrated public opinion. The tendency of modern democracy is for men to think alike, to feel alike, and to speak alike. Any departure from the conventional standards is apt to be regarded with suspicion. Public opinion is at once the chief safeguard of a democracy, and the chief menace to the real liberty of an individual. It almost seems as if the danger of despotism cannot be wholly averted under any form of government. In a political autocracy there is no effective public opinion, and all are subject to the tyranny of the ruler; in a democracy there is political freedom, but there is likely to be a tyranny of public opinion.
>
> An inviolable refuge from such tyranny should be found in the university. It should be an intellectual experiment station, where new ideas may germinate and where their fruit, though still distasteful to the community as a whole, may be allowed to ripen until finally, perchance, it may become part of the accepted intellectual food of the nation or of the world.

Declaration, supra note 12, at 297.

32. *Declaration, supra* note 12, at 294. Hence the conclusion of Thomas Haskell: "Historically speaking, the heart and soul of academic freedom lie not in free speech but in professional autonomy and collegial self-governance. Academic freedom came into being as a defense of the disciplinary community (or, more exactly, the

university conceived as an ensemble of such communities)." Thomas L. Haskell, *Justifying the Rights of Academic Freedom in the Era of "Power/Knowledge," in* THE FUTURE OF ACADEMIC FREEDOM 54 (Louis Menand, ed., 1996).

33. Note, *Academic Freedom and the Law,* 46 YALE. L.J. 670, 671 (1937).

34. The story is told in Van Alstyne, *supra* note 14. For a good discussion, see Walter P. Metzger, *Profession and Constitution: Two Definitions of Academic Freedom in America,* 66 TEX. L. REV. 1265 (1988); Paul Horwitz, Grutter's *First Amendment,* 46 B.C.L. REV. 461 (2005).

35. Keyishian v. Board of Regents, 385 U.S. 589, 603 (1967).

36. As Mark Yudof observed in 1987, "In my judgment, a persuasive constitutional argument for academic freedom as professorial autonomy has yet to emerge from the cases and scholarly works." Mark G. Yudof, *Three Faces of Academic Freedom,* 32 LOYOLA L. REV. 831, 838 (1987).

37. 354 U.S. 234 (1957).

38. *Id.* at 236.

39. *Id.* at 248.

40. *Id.* at 245.

41. *Id.* at 244.

42. On the importance of disciplinary standards to academic professionalism, see Emily M. Calhoun, *Academic Freedom: Disciplinary Lessons from Hogwarts,* 77 U. COLO. L. REV. 843 (2006).

43. *Sweezy,* 354 U.S. at 250. In the preceding paragraph Warren carefully distinguishes two distinct constitutional issues that correspond to the two distinct subjects of the Attorney General's investigation: "We believe that there unquestionably was an invasion of petitioner's liberties in the areas of academic freedom and political expression—areas in which government should be extremely reticent to tread." *Id.* Warren subsequently develops the theme of political liberty to engage in public discourse:

> Equally manifest as a fundamental principle of a democratic society is political freedom of the individual. Our form of government is built on the premise that every citizen shall

have the right to engage in political expression and association. This right was enshrined in the First Amendment of the Bill of Rights. Exercise of these basic freedoms in America has traditionally been through the media of political associations. Any interference with the freedom of a party is simultaneously an interference with the freedom of its adherents. All political ideas cannot and should not be channeled into the programs of our two major parties. History has amply proved the virtue of political activity by minority, dissident groups, who innumerable times have been in the vanguard of democratic thought and whose programs were ultimately accepted. Mere unorthodoxy or dissent from the prevailing mores is not to be condemned. The absence of such voices would be a symptom of grave illness in our society.

> *Id.* at 250–51.

44. *Id.* at 261–62 (Frankfurter, J., concurring).
45. *Id.* at 262–63 (Frankfurter, J., concurring). In his concurring opinion in *Wieman v. Updegraff,* 344 U.S. 183 (1952), which struck down a state statute requiring state employees to execute a loyalty oath, Frankfurter had already constructed the spine of an argument applicable to university faculty:

> The functions of educational institutions in our national life and the conditions under which alone they can adequately perform them are at the basis of these limitations upon State and national power. These functions and the essential conditions for their effective discharge have been well described by a leading educator:
>
>> Now, a university is a place that is established and will function for the benefit of society, provided it is a center of independent thought. It is a center of independent thought and criticism that is created in the interest of the progress of society, and the one reason that we know that every totalitarian government must fail is that no totalitarian government is prepared to face the consequences of creating free universities. . . .

> A university, then, is a kind of continuing Socratic
> conversation on the highest level for the very best people
> you can think of, you can bring together, about the most
> important questions, and the thing that you must do to
> the uttermost possible limits is to guarantee those men
> the freedom to think and to express themselves. . . .
>
> Statement of Robert M. Hutchins, Associate Director of the
> Ford Foundation, November 25, 1952, in Hearings before the
> House Select Committee to Investigate Tax-exempt Foun-
> dations and Comparable Organizations, pursuant to H.Res.
> 561, 82d Cong., 2d Sess.

Id. at 196–98 (Frankfurter, J., concurring).

46. Lovejoy, *supra* note 11.
47. For a discussion, see Post, *supra* note 10, at 74–79.
48. 438 U.S. 265, 311–13 (1978) (opinion of Powell, J.).
49. 539 U.S. 306, 329 (2003).
50. VANNEVAR BUSH, SCIENCE: THE ENDLESS FRONTIER; REPORT TO THE PRESIDENT ON A PROGRAM FOR POSTWAR SCIENTIFIC RESEARCH (1945).
51. *Id.* at 1.
52. *Id.* at 14.
53. *See* Robert Post, *Debating Disciplinarity,* 35 CRITICAL INQUIRY (2009). "Common sense identifies the term *discipline* with the content of an academic enterprise." David Shumway, *Disciplinarity, Corporatization, and the Crisis: A Dystopian Narrative,* J. MID-WEST MOD. LANGUAGE ASS'N, Winter-Spring 1999, at 2–18, 2.
54. Regents of Univ. of Mich. v. Ewing, 474 U.S. 214, 226 n.12 (1985) ("Academic freedom thrives not only on the independent and un-inhibited exchange of ideas among teachers and students . . . but also, and somewhat inconsistently, on autonomous decisionmak-ing by the academy itself"); Keen v. Penson, 970 F.2d 252, 257 (7th Cir. 1992) ("[A]s this case reveals, the assertion of academic freedom of a professor can conflict with the academic freedom of the university to make decisions affecting that professor"); Piar-owski v. Ill. Cmty. Coll. Dist. 525, 759 F.2d 625, 629 (7th Cir. 1985) ("[T]hough many decisions describe 'academic freedom' as an

aspect of the freedom of speech that is protected against governmental abridgment by the First Amendment, . . . the term is equivocal. It is used to denote both the freedom of the academy to pursue its ends without interference from the government (the sense in which it is used, for example, in Justice Powell's opinion in *Regents of the University of California v. Bakke,* 438 U.S. 265, 312 (1978), or in our recent decision in *EEOC v. University of Notre Dame Du Lac,* 715 F.2d 331, 335–36 (7th Cir.1983)), and the freedom of the individual teacher (or in some versions—indeed in most cases—the student) to pursue his ends without interference from the academy; and these two freedoms are in conflict, as in this case."); Dow Chem. Co. v. Allen, 672 F.2d 1262, 1275 (7th Cir. 1982) ("Case law considering the standard to be applied where the issue is academic freedom of the university to be free of governmental interference, as opposed to academic freedom of the individual teacher to be free of restraints from the university administration, is surprisingly sparse."); Cooper v. Ross, 472 F.Supp. 802, 813 (D.C. Ark. 1979) ("The present case is particularly difficult because it involves a fundamental tension between the academic freedom of the individual teacher to be free of restraints from the university administration, and the academic freedom of the university to be free of government, including judicial, interference.").

55. Byrne, *supra* note 2; J. Peter Byrne, *The Threat to Constitutional Academic Freedom,* 31 J.C. & U.L. 79 (2004); Alan K. Chen, *Bureaucracy and Distrust: Germaneness and the Paradoxes of Academic Freedom Doctrine,* 77 U. Colo. L. Rev. 955 (2006); Richard H. Hiers, *Institutional Academic Freedom vs. Faculty Academic Freedom in Public Colleges and Universities,* 29 31 J.C. & U.L. 35 (2002); Richard H. Hiers, *Institutional Academic Freedom or Autonomy Grounded Upon the First Amendment: A Jurisprudential Mirage,* 30 Hamline L. Rev. 1 (2007); Matthew Finkin, *On "Institutional" Academic Freedom,* 61 Tex. L. Rev. 817 (1983); Rachel Fugate, *Choppy Waters Are Forecast for Academic Free Speech,* 26 Fla. St. U.L. Rev. 187 (1998); Erica Goldberg and Kelly Sarabyn, *Measuring a "Degree of Difference": Institutional Academic Freedom in a Post-*Grutter *World,* 51 Santa Clara L. Rev. 217, 217–19 (2011); Elizabeth Mertz, *The Burden of Proof and Academic Freedom:*

Protection for Institution or Individual?, 82 Nw. U.L. Rev. 292
(1988); Michael A. Olivas, *Reflections on Professorial Academic
Freedom: Second Thoughts on the Third "Essential Freedom,"* 45
Stan. L. Rev. 1835 (1993); David M. Rabban, *Functional Analysis
of "Individual" and "Institutional" Academic Freedom Under the
First Amendment,* 53 Law & Contemp. Probs. 227 (Summer 1990);
Frederick Schauer, *Is There a Right to Academic Freedom?* 77 U.
Colo. L. Rev. 907 (2006); Yudof, *supra* note 36, at 853–57.

56. I do not here consider the dimensions of academic freedom that
    concern freedom to teach or freedom of extramural speech.

57. Eliot, *supra* note 30, at 1–2.

58. *Declaration, supra* note 12, at 293.

59. *Id.*

60. As Kant observes, "The university would have a certain auton-
    omy (since only scholars can pass judgment on scholars as such)."
    Kant, *supra* note 29, at 23.

61. Carley v. Ariz. Bd. of Regents, 737 P.2d 1099, 1102 (Ariz. App. 1987).

62. Regents of the Univ. of Mich. v. Ewing, 474 U.S. 214, 225 (1985).
    See Bd. of Curators, Univ. of Mo. v. Horowitz, 435 U.S. 78, 90–92
    (1978); *id.* at 96 n.6 (opinion of Powell, J., concurring); Clark v.
    Whiting, 607 F.2d 634 (4th Cir. 1979); Brown v. George Washing-
    ton Univ., 802 A.2d 382, 385 (D.C. 2002).

63. Bishop v. Aronov, 92 F.2d 1066, 1075 (11th Cir. 1991).

64. *See, e.g.,* Judith Areen, *Government as Educator: A New Under-
    standing of First Amendment Protection of Academic Freedom and
    Governance,* 97 Geo. L.J. 945, 994–99 (2009).

65. *Declaration, supra* note 12, at 294.

66. For a discussion of when judicial deference may or may not be
    appropriate when using the First Amendment to review insti-
    tutional decision-making, see Robert Post, *Between Management
    and Governance: The History and Theory of the Public Forum,* 34
    UCLA L. Rev. 1713 (1987).

67. 216 F.3d 401 (4th Cir. 2000).

68. *Id.* at 404.

69. *Id.* at 411.

70. *Id.* at 412. "The Court has focused its discussions of academic free-
    dom solely on issues of institutional autonomy." *Id.* at 415.

71. The Court also failed to realize that the Virginia statute was in fact a regulation of the university itself. *See* Byrne, *supra* note 55, at 112. *Gilmore* should be compared to *Henley v. Wise*, 303 F.Supp. 62, 66 (D.C. Ind. 1969), which struck down an Indiana statute criminalizing the possession of obscene material without intent to sell, lend, or give away, in part because the statute "intruded" into "the right of scholars to do research and advance the state of man's knowledge."

72. *Gilmore*, 216 F.3d at 415.

73. 319 U.S. 563 (1968).

74. 461 U.S. 138 (1983).

75. 511 U.S. 661 (1994).

76. *Connick*, 461 U.S. at 146–47.

77. Trejo v. Shoben, 319 F.3d 878 (7th Cir. 2003); Bonnell v. Lorenzo, 241 F.3d 800 (6th Cir. 2001); Hardy v. Jefferson Cmty. Coll., 260 F.3d 671 (6th Cir. 2001); Dambrot v. Central Michigan University, 55 F.3d 1177 (6th Cir. 1995); Jeffries v. Harleston, 52 F.3d 9 (2d Cir. 1995); Blum v. Schlegel, 18 F.3d 1005 (2d Cir. 1994); Hong v. Grant, 516 F.Supp.2d 1158 (C.D. CA. 2007), *aff'd*, 403 Fed. App'x. 236 (9th Cir. 2010); Scallet v. Rosenblum, 911 F.Supp. 999, 1009–14 (W.D. Va. 1996); Rubin v. Ikenberry, 933 F.Supp. 1425 (C.D. Ill. 1996); Silva v. University of New Hampshire, 888 F. Supp. 293 (D.N.H. 1994); Ailsa W. Chang, *Resuscitating the Constitutional "Theory" of Academic Freedom: A Search for a Standard Beyond Pickering and* Connick, 53 STAN. L. REV. 915 (2001); Edgar Dyer, *Collegiality's Potential Chill Over Faculty Speech: Demonstrating the Need for a Refined Version of* Pickering and Connick *for Public Higher Education*, 119 EDUC. L. REP. 309 (1997); Jennifer Elrod, *Academics, Public Employee Speech, and the Public University*, 22 BUFF. PUB. INT. L.J. 1 (2003–2004); Richard H. Hiers, *Academic Freedom in Public Colleges and Universities: O Say, Does that Star-Spangled First Amendment Banner Yet Wave?*, 40 WAYNE L. REV. 1 (1993); Chris Hoofnagle, *Matters of Public Concern and the Public University Professor*, 27 J.C. & U.L. 669 (2001); Robert J. Tepper, *Speak No Evil: Academic Freedom and the Application of* Garcetti v. Ceballos *to the Public University Faculty*, 59 CATH. U.L. REV. 125, 129 (2009).

78. *See* Areen, *supra* note 64, at 975–76.
79. The logic of this and the following paragraph is developed in detail in Post, *supra* note 66.
80. *Pickering,* 391 U.S. at 568.
81. *Connick,* 461 U.S. at 142.
82. *Id.* Immanuel Kant early on identified this tension. In *An Answer to the Question: "What Is Enlightenment?"* he observes:

> The *public* use of man's reason must always be free. . . . the *private use* of reason may quite often be very narrowly restricted. . . . [B]y the public use of one's own reason I mean that use which anyone may make of it *as a man of learning* addressing the entire *reading public.* What I term the private use of reason is that which a person may make of it in a particular *civil* post or office with which he is entrusted.
>
> Now in some affairs which affect the interests of the commonwealth, we require a certain mechanism whereby some members of the commonwealth must behave purely passively, so that they may, by an artificial common agreement, be employed by the government for public ends. . . . It is, of course, impermissible to argue in such cases; obedience is imperative. But in so far as this or that individual who acts as part of the machine also considers himself as a member of a complete commonwealth or even of cosmopolitan society, and thence as a man of learning who may through his writings address a public in the truest sense of the word, he may indeed argue without harming the affairs in which he is employed for some of the time in a passive capacity. Thus it would be very harmful if an officer receiving an order from his superiors were to quibble openly, while on duty, about the appropriateness or usefulness of the order in question. He must simply obey. But he cannot reasonably be banned from making observations as a man of learning on the errors in the military service, and from submitting these to his public for judgement.

IMMANUEL KANT, POLITICAL WRITINGS 55–56 (Hans Reiss ed., H. B. Nisbet trans., 1991).

83. Yudof, *supra* note 36, at 838–40; Robert Post, *Racist Speech, Democracy, and the First Amendment*, 32 WM & MARY L. REV. 267, 317–25 (1990).

84. *Sweezy*, 354 U.S. at 250. For a discussion see *supra* notes 37–43.

85. Indeed, the *1915 Declaration* specifically states that "the classroom utterances of college and university teachers" should "always . . . be considered privileged communications. Discussions in the classroom ought not to be supposed to be utterances for the public at large." *1915 Declaration, supra* note 12, at 299.

86. *See supra* notes 15–16.

87. *1940 Statement*, quoted in note 16 *supra*.

88. See, in this regard, the remarks of Harvard President Abbott Lawrence Lowell:

> [T]he right of a professor to express his views without restraint on matters lying outside the sphere of his professorship is not a question of academic freedom in its true sense, but of the personal liberty of the citizen. It has nothing to do with liberty of research and instruction in the subject for which the professor occupies the chair that makes him a member of the university. The fact that a man fills a chair of astronomy, for example, confers on him no special knowledge of, and no peculiar right to speak upon, the protective tariff. His right to speak about a subject on which he is not an authority is simply the right of any other man, and the question is simply whether the university or college by employing him as a professor acquires a right to restrict his freedom as a citizen.

Quoted in HENRY AARON YEOMANS, ABBOTT LAWRENCE LOWELL, 1856–1943, at 310 (1948).

89. An example would be the case of Sami Al-Arian, a computer science professor who was disciplined for statements concerning terrorism in the Middle East after September 11, 2001. *See* Joe Humphrey, *Professors Condemn Al-Arian's Firing*, TAMPA TRIB., June 15, 2003, at 1. For the AAUP investigative report on the Al-Arian case, see 89 ACADEME, No. 3, at 59 (2003).

90. For a discussion, *see* FINKIN AND POST, *supra* note 24; William W.

Van Alstyne, *The Specific Theory of Academic Freedom and the General Issue of Civil Liberties*, 404 Annals Am. Acad. Pol. & Soc. Sci. 140, 146–47 (1972):

> The phrase "academic freedom," in the context "the academic freedom of a faculty member of an institution of higher learning" refers to a set of vocational liberties: to teach, to investigate, to do research, and to publish on any subject as a matter of professional interest, without vocational jeopardy or threat of other sanction, save only upon adequate demonstration of an inexcusable breach of professional ethics in the exercise of any of them. Specifically, that which sets academic freedom apart as a distinct freedom is its vocational claim of special and limited accountability in respect to all academically related pursuits of the teacher-scholar: an accountability not to any institutional or societal standard of economic benefit, acceptable interest, right thinking, or socially constructive theory, but solely to a fiduciary standard of professional integrity. To condition the employment or personal freedom of the teacher-scholar upon the institutional or societal approval of his academic investigations or utterances, or to qualify either even by the immediate impact of his professional endeavors upon the economic well-being or good will of the very institution which employs him, is to abridge his academic freedom. The maintenance of academic freedom contemplates an accountability in respect to academic investigations and utterances solely in respect of their professional integrity, a matter usually determined by reference to professional ethical standards of truthful disclosure and reasonable care.

Van Alstyne explicitly contrasts academic freedom to the civil liberties protected by extramural speech: "The legitimate claims of personal autonomy possessed equally by all persons, wholly without reference to academic freedom, frame a distinct and separate set of limitations upon the just power of an institution to use its leverage of control." *Id.* at 146. At the time of the *1940 Statement*, before the demise of the rights/privilege distinction, First Amendment doctrine did not extend civil liberty to participate in public discourse to government employees.

91. *See* Rebecca Gose Lynch, *Pawns of the State or Priests of Democracy: Analyzing Professors' Academic Freedom Rights Within the State's Managerial Realm*, 91 CALIF. L. REV. 1061 (2003). Because sanctions against university administrators in their administrative capacities may not involve the constitutional value of democratic competence, the deployment of the "public concern" test in such circumstances is far more defensible than its use to assess the academic freedom of tenured faculty in their work as scholars. *See, e.g.*, Schrier v. Univ. of Colo., 427 F.3d 1253 (10th Cir. 2005); Jeffries v. Harlseton, 52 F.3d 9 (2d Cir. 1995).

92. 484 U.S. 260 (1988). "The most commonly applied tests are variations of one sort or another of what we have called the Hazelwood test and the Pickering-Connick-Garcetti or PCG test." Wright, *supra* note 5, at 816. *See* Axson-Flynn v. Johnson, 356 F.3d 1277 (10th Cir. 2004); Scallet v. Rosenblum, 911 F. Supp. 999, 1010 (W.D. Va. 1996).

93. 926 F.2d 1066 (11th Cir. 1991).

94. *Id.* at 1074.

95. *Id.* at 1075.

96. *See supra* notes 15–16.

97. For a discussion of this tension, see *Piggee v. Carl Sandburg College*, 464 F.3d 667, 670–71 (7th Cir. 2006).

98. Wieman v. Updegraff, 344 U.S. 183, 196–98 (1952) (Frankfurter, J., concurring).

99. AMY GUTMANN, DEMOCRATIC EDUCATION (1987). *See* BENJAMIN R. BARBER, AN ARISTOCRACY OF EVERYONE: THE POLITICS OF EDUCATION AND THE FUTURE OF AMERICA 15 (1992) ("[I]n democracies, education is the indispensable concomitant of citizenship.").

100. Court decisions have sometimes analyzed student rights in primary and secondary schools on the assumption that the constitutional purpose of public education is to produce democratically competent students, and they have sometimes analyzed such rights on the quite distinct assumption that the constitutional purpose of public education is to reproduce existing cultural values. *Compare* Tinker v. Des Moines School Dist., 393 U.S. 503 (1969), *with*

Bethel v. School Dist. No. 403 v. Frazer, 478 U.S. 675 (1986). For a discussion, see Robert Post, *Racist Speech, Democracy, and the First Amendment*, 32 Wm. & Mary L. Rev. 267, 317–25 (1990).

101. Nor do I address academic freedom to engage in so-called intramural speech, which concerns matters of internal university governance. *See* Areen, *supra* note 64.

102. *Aronov*, 926 F.2d at 1068.

103. I am not now considering cases in which university administrators seek to limit the ability of faculty to report the conclusions of their research to students on the ground that expressing such conclusions would undermine the pedagogical mission of the university. In contrast to *Sweezy*, universities in such cases do not pre-judge the truth of questions under classroom consideration; they instead assert a conflict between the heuristic mission of the university and its scholarly mission. Such conflicts might sometimes be said to arise in the context of racist or sexist speech, where it has been argued that reports of scholarly conclusions would undermine the ability of students to learn. In such circumstances the academic freedom of faculty to report pedagogically pertinent scholarly conclusions is conceded; at issue are the reasons that might justify circumscribing that freedom.

104. *See supra* note 58.

105. Dewey, *supra* note 9.

106. 547 U.S. 410 (2006).

107. *Id.* at 421.

108. Mayer v. Monroe County Community School Corp., 474 F.3d 477, 479 (7th Cir. 2007). Yudof observes that "[u]nless an abridgement of speech lies in every exercise of governmental authority to speak through individuals—and how else might abstract entities called governments speak?—it is difficult to countenance the view that government control of its own professional speakers violates the historically developed concepts of freedom of expression." Yudof, *supra* note 36, at 839.

109. Renken v. Gregory, 541 F.3d 769, 773 (7th Cir. 2008). *See, e.g.,* Capeheart v. Hahs, Slip Copy, 2011 WL 657848 (N.D. Ill. 2011); Isenalumhe v. McDuffie, 697 F.Supp.2d 367 (E.D.N.Y. 2010); Miller v. Univ. of S. Ala., Slip Copy, 2010 WL 1994910 (S.D. Ala. 2010);

Sadid v. Idaho State Univ., Slip Copy, No. CV-2008-3942-OC, (Idaho 6th Jud. Dist. Dec. 18, 2009). *But see* Kerr v. Hurd, 694 F.Supp.2d 817, 843–44 (S.D. Ohio 2010); Sheldon v. Bilbir Dhillon, Slip Copy, 2009 WL 4282086 (N.D. Cal. 2009). *See also* Adams v. Trustees of the UNCW, Slip Copy, No. 10-1413 (4th Cir. Apr. 6, 2011); Savage v. Gee, 716 F.Supp.2d 709 (S.D. Ohio 2010); Gorum v. Sessoms, 561 F.3d 179 (3d Cir. 2009); Tepper, *supra* note 77.

110. *Garcetti,* 547 U.S. at 425.
111. *Declaration, supra* note 12, at 295.
112. *Id. See* Matthew Finkin, *Intramural Speech, Academic Freedom, and the First Amendment,* 66 TEX. L. REV. 1323, 1337–38 (1988).

Conclusion

1. FRANCIS BACON, THE ESSAIES (*"Of Heresies"*) np (1613).
2. FRANCIS BACON, ESSAYS WITH ANNOTATIONS BY RICHARD WHATELY 577 (1868). Bacon writes:

   Printing, a gross invention; artillery, a thing that lay not far out of the way; the needle, a thing partly known before: what a change have these three made in the world in these times; the one in a state of learning, the other in state of the war, the third in the state of treasure, commodities, and navigation!

   Id.
3. T. S. ELIOT, *choruses from "The Rock,"* in THE COMPLETE POEMS AND PLAYS 1909–1950 96 (1962).
4. *See* text at Chapter One, note 1.
5. The South Dakota case is discussed in Robert Post, *Informed Consent to Abortion: A First Amendment Analysis of Compelled Physician Speech,* 2007 ILL. L. REV. 939; the Nebraska case in Planned Parenthood v. Heineman, 724 F.Supp.2nd 1025, 1048 (D. Neb.2010). Al Kamen, *Backlash Brewing,* WASH. POST, February 10, 2006, at A17; *Censoring Truth,* N.Y. TIMES, February 9, 2006, at 26.
6. Joan W. Scott, *Academic Freedom as an Ethical Practice, in* THE FUTURE OF ACADEMIC FREEDOM 175 (Louis Menand ed., 1996).

7. For a nice summary of the insights of cultural and sociological studies of these aspects of science, see David Caudill, *Law, Science, and Science Studies: Contrasting the Deposition of a Scientific Expert with Ethnographic Studies of Scientific Practice,* 12 S. CAL. INTERDISC. L.J. 88 (2002).

8. Milton and Rose Friedman, for example, famously argued in 1962 that

> licensure is the key to the medical profession's . . . ability to restrict technological and organizational changes in the way medicine is conducted. The American Medical Association has been consistently against the practice of group medicine, and against prepaid medical plans. . . . [T]he medical association is against only one type of group practice, namely, prepaid group practice. The economic reason seems to be that this eliminates the possibility of engaging in discriminatory pricing.

MILTON FRIEDMAN & ROSE D. FRIEDMAN, CAPITALISM AND FREEDOM 154–55 (2d ed. 1982). Contemporary critics of the healthcare system have argued that new technology for determining eyeglass prescriptions has been stymied because it threatens eye doctors, and that physicians' assistants have not been granted responsibility commensurate with their ability because of "the predictable desire of physicians to preserve their traditional market hegemony." Clayton M. Christensen et al., *Will Disruptive Innovations Cure Health Care?,* HARV. BUS. REV., Sept.–Oct. 2000, at 107–8.

9. ANTHONY GIDDENS, BEYOND LEFT AND RIGHT: THE FUTURE OF RADICAL POLITICS 128 (1994).

10. *Id.* at 131.

Index